"Great Brands simply make a promise and then keep that promise. You make promises through advertising, promotion and sponsorships. Beyond Philosophy's unique proprietary methodologies help you deliver on your promise ruthlessly and consistently across every consumer touch point." – **Gary Keogh**, *Marketing Manager, Glenfiddich*

"If you have anything to do with Customer Experience you must read this book. It shows the future! Beyond Philosophy = Thought leadership." – **Darren Cornish**, *Head of Customer Intelligence, Customer Experience, Axa Insurance*

"I get a lot of companies wanting to talk to me about Customer Experience. There is only one company I would talk to, the Thought Leaders, Beyond Philosophy. Why accept second best?" – **Bob Black**, *Managing Director, TNT, Australia*

"We have worked with Beyond Philosophy for a number of years. Why? This book reinforces why. They are Thought Leaders and understand Customer's emotional drivers." – **Laree R. Daniel**, *Senior Vice President, Customer Assurance Organization, Aflac*

"Once again Beyond Philosophy demonstrate their thought leadership in the field of Customer Experience. An insightful book which shows us the future." – **Charmaine McDonald**, *Senior Vice President, Customer Success (Clinical Solutions), McKesson*

"For the past five years we have successfully focussed on improving our Customer Experience with the help and guidance of Beyond Philosophy. This book outlines the next steps of the journey." – **Steve Elliott**, *Managing Director, Morgan Sindall*

"Beyond Philosophy have been pioneers in defining the Customer Experience. This book reinforces their Thought Leadership position. It is a must read!" – **Ivan Mainprize**, *VP Customer Experience, Membership Travel Services International, American Express*

CUSTOMER EXPERIENCE
FUTURE TRENDS AND INSIGHTS

Also by Colin Shaw and published by Palgrave Macmillan:

The DNA of Customer Experience
Revolutionize Your Customer Experience
Building Great Customer Experiences (with John Ivens)

Customer Experience
Future Trends and Insights

Colin Shaw
Founder and CEO, Beyond Philosophy

Qaalfa Dibeehi
Chief Operating and Consulting Officer,
Beyond Philosophy

Steven Walden
Senior Head of Research and Consulting,
Beyond Philosophy

palgrave
macmillan

First published 2010 by
PALGRAVE MACMILLAN

Palgrave Macmillan in the UK is an imprint of Macmillan Publishers Limited, registered in England, company number 785998, of Houndmills, Basingstoke, Hampshire RG21 6XS.

Palgrave Macmillan in the US is a division of St Martin's Press LLC, 175 Fifth Avenue, New York, NY 10010.

Palgrave Macmillan is the global academic imprint of the above companies and has companies and representatives throughout the world.

Palgrave® and Macmillan® are registered trademarks in the United States, the United Kingdom, Europe and other countries

ISBN 978-0-230-24781-9

This book is printed on paper suitable for recycling and made from fully managed and sustained forest sources. Logging, pulping and manufacturing processes are expected to conform to the environmental regulations of the country of origin.

A catalogue record for this book is available from the British Library.

A catalog record for this book is available from the Library of Congress.

10 9 8 7 6 5 4 3 2
19 18 17 16 15 14 13 12 11 10

Printed and bound in Great Britain by
CPI Antony Rowe, Chippenham and Eastbourne

Contents

Figures and tables

Figures

Figures and Tables

Tables

Foreword

The next time you are travelling down the road, look out for the containers on trucks that are being transported around the countryside. The chances are you will see the Maersk star on one of them; this will be one of our containers being delivered or picking up some cargo. Maersk Line is the world's largest container shipping line, with a market share of 15 percent and approximately 500 vessels operated, represented in 130+ countries, with around 17,000 employees.

By its very nature, the container shipping business is a very logical, logistical and thus a left-brain business. Using a word like "emotion" has not been a common occurrence. This is part of our challenge.

I have come to the realization that businesses today are obsessed with gaining efficiencies without looking at the wider picture. Now, clearly I am not saying that being efficient is not important. Far from it, it is very important. However, it is not the final answer. In today's world you need to run an efficient business AND focus on the customer. It is not either/or, it is both. In focusing on the customer, it is important to realize that customers are people, and as such they are driven by emotions. I have always felt that there was much more to a Customer Experience than just providing customers with "what" they wanted, critically it is also about "how" this is done. We quickly reached the realization we needed to improve our Customer Experience and move it onto a new, improved level for our customers, and in so doing this would provide us with differentiation. In addition, we recognized we didn't have all the answers and needed to collaborate with some experts.

When we started to engage with Beyond Philosophy a number of aspects started to come together. They made us realize that we needed to focus more on customer emotions. They taught us that over 50 percent of a Customer Experience is about emotions, even in a business to business environment. As they are outlining in this book, they taught us that we needed to look "under the skin" of what customers are saying to truly understand their motivations, desires, and what drives value. In short, I recognized that we needed to examine what customers really want, at a much deeper level than we were doing. How to do that is outlined in this book.

Their approach takes a complex subject and makes it simple. They have helped us define our strategy for Maersk's Customer Experience and provided us with a number of tools that we can use to enhance it. The great thing for a logical, left-brain organization is that they put some science behind the art of the Customer Experience. Specifically, their Emotional Signature® methodology, referred to in this book, has been fundamental in our approach. It shows the subconscious parts of a customer's experience and informs you of the areas that you should focus on to improve your Customer Experience and critically what drives the most value.

When I was subsequently asked to write the forward for this book I was more than happy to do so.

In our hearts we all know that we need to understand the customer much better than we do, and in my view that means we need to get into the psychological aspects of a Customer Experience. All businesses need to truly understand what makes the customer tick, not just at a superficial level as most research seems to do. This book outlines how this can be done.

I have the great pleasure of commending this book to you. Oh, and when you pass the driver of the container lorry as you drive down the road, give him a wave, he's carrying some of our customers' cargo, and that is the most important job in the world to us!

Hanne B. Sørensen
Chief Commercial Officer
Maersk Line

Acknowledgments

From the authors

Writing a book in the midst of the worst recession for decades is probably not the best idea we have ever had!

It has, however, turned out well, as we are proud to say we have built a great team at Beyond Philosophy. We would like to take this opportunity to acknowledge the team for their help in getting this book to market. Thank you to David Ive, Zhecho Dobrev, Kalina Janevska, Tami Rehmert, Greg Rutledge, Suzanne Smart, Vally Smith, Rebeca Miranda, Derek Blackburn, John Adedoyin, and Sue Morgan, to name a few.

Thanks to Bob Thompson of Customer Think (www.customerthink. com) for his help with the social media research.

We would also like to thank a number of our clients who have been kind enough to contribute to this book. As always their support is much appreciated.

Colin Shaw's acknowledgments

Thanks to Kalina Janevska and Rebeca Miranda for their help on the research of my part of the book.

I have mentioned many people in the last three books so I intended to keep this quite short. To my friends Graham, Hazel, Dave, Bernadette, Paul, Anne, Martin, Laraine, Stuart, Brian, and Sue. Without giving them a mention, my life would be hell for the next 10 years! Also to my Dad and my brother Neil.

As usual at my right hand is my wife Lorraine, ever present, ever supportive, ever encouraging and probably most importantly, always understanding. Without her constant backing I would not have been able to enjoy the amazing adventure that establishing Beyond Philosophy has been. I would especially like to thank my adult children, Coralie, Ben, and Abbie. I am incredibly proud of each of them. I dedicate my part of the book to them. Kids, "I love you all the buttons in the world."

Qaalfa Dibeehi's acknowledgments

A nostalgic thanks to Dr. Phillip Ramsey for sparking my intellectual curiosity in statistics and mathematical psychology all those years back, and Dr. David Morse for giving me early direction in psychobiology. A personal thanks to a few of my colleagues, Zhecho Dobrev, Kalina Janevska, and Rebeca Miranda, whose ideas are always enlightening. Thanks to friends who have challenged my thinking; Carmen Alonso, Christa Bynam, Karolina Grajek, Harold Hodges, Yumiko Ogawa, Rie Sasaki, and Richard Sheahan. A heartfelt thanks to mom for her unending support and my big bro', Rock, who I still idolize. And to Dr. Denise Barrett, we did it together. Finally, a long lost thanks to Diana and Alina.

Steven Walden's acknowledgments

My thanks to the following for their advice guidance and support: Dr. Nigel Marlow, Professor Hugh Wilson, Dr. Pete Jones, Professor Gemma Calvert, Dr. Mark Johnson, Dr. Emma MacDonald, Darren Howden, Samir Savant, Lorraine Grubbs-West, Maxine Clark, Steve Elliott, Rob Frank, and Don Buckley, as well as all those in Beyond Philosophy who read various drafts and provided advice and guidance (Zhecho, Kalina, Rebeca, and Suzanne). Not forgetting my partner Rachel and our two children Lorna and Lydia who had to put up with a summer of writing.

About the authors

Colin Shaw

Colin Shaw is the Founder & CEO of Beyond Philosophy®, the world's thought leaders in Customer Experience.

Colin is a successful international author of three best-selling books, *Building Great Customer Experiences* (2002), *Revolutionize Your Customer Experience* (2004), and *The DNA of Customer Experience: How Emotions Drive Value* (2007), all published by Palgrave Macmillan.

He has spent over 20 years working in blue-chip organizations, in many different functions including sales, marketing, training, and customer service. His corporate career culminated in his appointment as Senior Vice President of Customer Experience for one of the world's largest companies, where he led 3,500 people across the globe.

In foreseeing the emergence of Customer Experience as a new market, Colin left the security of the corporate world to establish, in 2002, the Beyond Philosophy consultancy, research, and training company which is solely focused on the Customer Experience. He started working from home and has built Beyond Philosophy to what it is today, recognized as thought leaders in Customer Experience, with offices in London, England, Atlanta, USA, and partners in Europe and Asia.

Beyond Philosophy is proud to have worked with many of the world's largest organizations, including American Express, Microsoft, IBM, Aviva, Royal Bank of Scotland, and Allianz to name just a few.

Colin knows what makes businesses tick. He understands the importance of theories and strategy, but ultimately knows it's about getting things done. Colin's practical approach, born from his operational background, is highly valued by clients.

Owing to his expertise, Colin has appeared as a commentator many times on television, including CNN and the BBC. He is a sought-after and accomplished public speaker, delivering thought-provoking keynote speeches around the globe. He is a member of the National Speakers Association.

Qaalfa Dibeehi

Qaalfa Dibeehi is Chief Operating and Consulting Officer at Beyond Philosophy. He has 18 years senior-level experience in the customer strategy space in the United States, Europe, and Asia. He was formerly an award-winning professor and an experienced public speaker. He can periodically be found on television (Sky News, BBC, ITN) commenting on topical business issues as seen through the Customer Experience lens.

He is particularly interested in the special problems and sensitivities of organizations that have a dual commercial and social/community responsibility. His focus is on the business implications (as opposed to the positive psychology) of Customer Experience, especially the over-looked impact of our subconscious, emotional and neuro-experience on business value. He prefers to get in there and mix it up with the tough but necessary decisions managers and executives have to make in order to make Customer Experience a reality.

Qaalfa is able to draw on best practice from a wide variety of fields and sectors based on his personal experiences. His previous experi-ence includes senior roles at Fulcrum Analytics where he was Director of the Consumer and Strategy consulting practices in New York and London respectively. He was managing consultant at Round, the customer centricity firm, where he helped develop an assessment tool that eventually won the 2003 CRM Innovation of the Year award. He has also run two specialist consultancies, Jacques Quant Partners, which focused on NYC's design (fashion and architecture) sector, and Counterpoint3, a London-based strategic CRM partnership. He has held strategic planning and analysis roles with Schering-Plough Phar-maceuticals and Citibank. In the early 1990s Qaalfa worked for the City of New York, where he was responsible for medical, physical, and psychological occupational health standards.

Qaalfa has a broad-based but deep education with four Master's degrees. He has an MBA (international business and management) from New York University and Master's degrees in Statistics, Psychology, and Health Administration from the City University of New York. He graduated with departmental distinction in Psychobiology from the State University of New York. He also has an ABD in neuropsychology from City University of New York.

True to his nomadic trans-Saharan ancestry, Qaalfa is a world traveler, and has lived and worked in the three of the world's great cities (NYC, London, and Tokyo). He would have been recruited for professional basketball were it not for his lack of talent.

Steven Walden

Steven has 14 years of management consultancy experience focused on consumer-facing research and insights. He is Beyond Philosophy's Senior Head of Research and Consulting. Prior to working at Beyond Philosophy he worked at several major consulting organizations, project managing for many blue-chip clients, engagements concerned with business to consumer and business to business market strategies.

Steven has a Master's in Strategic Marketing with Customer Market Research, focusing on segmentation methodologies. With an interest in understanding the emotional and subconscious side of the Customer Experience, Steven has been instrumental in developing ground-breaking methodologies such as Emotional Signature®. He is a regular 'blogger' on the Market Research Society website.

With strong links to several leading business schools, speaking at several leading Customer Experience events, Steven bridges the gap between academic thinking and the practical application of Customer Experience Management.

Steven is a leading expert on the use of psychology in Customer Experience Management and is a recognized expert in understanding how to use the emotions and subconscious mind of clients and consumers to generate value and the application of value-in-use to experience.

A highly engaging and professional speaker, Steven Walden brings the topic of Customer Experience to life through his extensive knowledge.

Beyond Philosophy can be contacted at:

UK & Worldwide Office:
180 Piccadilly
London W1J 9HG
+44 (0)207 917 1717

North American Office
Suite 700
One Glenlake Parkway
Atlanta
Georgia 30328
(+1)-678 638 6162

Web & blog sites: www.beyondphilosophy.com

1 Reflections of the authors, Colin, Qaalfa and Steven …

We remember:

- when Colin's wife Lorraine said, "Why would I want to have a mobile phone or use email?"
- when mobile phones were so small they could fit in an attaché case
- when the remote control was the kids!
- when lemonade soda was delivered to your front door
- using a payphone
- when no car had air conditioning
- not having the internet
- not having a computer at home or at work
- photocopying memos to share with the team
- being in the queue in the 1970s when the first McDonald's opened in London, England
- when supermarkets were a new concept
- typing pools at work
- when there was no such thing as political correctness
- when kids played in the street
- when the insurance man used to collect your money from your house
- black and white television
- when you didn't have to wear seat belts in a car
- when writing a check made out to yourself was the only way to get cash from the bank
- when it was a big deal that a calculator didn't require batteries – solar power had arrived
- when music portability went from vinyl 45s to eight-track to cassette tapes to CDs
- when you bought an extra-long cord for the phone so you could speak with some privacy in the other room.

How times change. It is amazing to think of all the things that have changed over our lifetime, and we are sure you could add to this list.

In the early 1970s if someone had told us that most people would have a cellphone and this could allow you to watch television or a video as you walk down the street, and you could also view satellite images of anywhere in the world, all free of charge, you would have thought them mad. How times have changed.

In 2002 we started Beyond Philosophy, a niche consultancy and specialized research company focusing only on the Customer Experience. It's fun to reflect back on those days. At the time, we were amongst the first pioneers of the Customer Experience, following Pine and Gilmore's seminal book *The Experience Economy.* At the time many people had not really considered what a Customer Experience was, let alone understood it. We spent a great deal of our time educating people on what this really means, and we still do so today. However sitting here today, writing this, we realize eight years later how times have changed.

What were you doing eight years ago? Have you learned a lot over that time? We are sure you have. The same applies with us. For the past eight years all we have focused on is the Customer Experience and helping clients around the globe to build great Customer Experiences – oh, and writing four books on the subject!

As you can imagine, what we have learned is quite amazing. Over the years, we have undertaken countless research studies, and have had many successes as well as a few failures. For us this is OK as we live life by this quote from Theodore Roosevelt, 26th president of the United States:

> Far better it is to dare mighty things, to win glorious triumphs even though chequered by failure, than to rank with those poor spirits who neither enjoy nor suffer much, because they live in the gray twilight that knows neither victory nor defeat.

Sometime when you fail, you learn more than if you succeed. With all this experience we have a pretty good idea of what works and what doesn't. For example we now know:

- Customer Experience is far more about the emotional side of the Customer Experience than people recognize.
- Many people don't understand that.
- It is CRITICAL to understand customers much more deeply than most organizations do.
- It is fundamental to design a deliberate experience.
- You need to define the experience that you want to deliver.

- You need to find out what customers really want, not what they tell you at a superficial level.
- Senior managers will want to understand the impact on value, in pounds, dollars, and so on.
- You need to focus on the things that drive or destroy value to get the win/win of improving the experience for the customer and gaining more profit.
- The Web and social media are changing everything.
- People in the business to business environment think this doesn't apply to them, when it does.
- Research shows that a business to business experience has the same basic ingredients as a business to consumer experience, as in both cases we are dealing with people!
- Many more things!

In this book we shall address a number of these issues, and more. From our research and discussions with forward-thinking clients, academia, and industry analysts, we shall reveal to you the emerging trends in Customer Experience. As with any predictions, we are certain we will get some right and some wrong. However, to a degree, we are also living by what Alan Kay observed:

The best way to predict the future is to invent it.

As our learning has increased, so we have needed to enhance previous thinking. The definition of a Customer Experience is a case in point. We believe we now need to change this from the one we gave in our last book. This will be our third revision over eight years. Our new definition of a Customer Experience is:

A Customer Experience is an interaction between an organization and a customer as perceived through a customer's conscious and subconscious mind. It is a blend of an organization's rational performance, the senses stimulated and emotions evoked, and intuitively measured against customer expectations across all moments of contact.

We are not going to go into this, as we have done so in previous books. Suffice it to say that we know over 50 percent of a Customer Experience is about emotions: in other words, how a customer feels. The only way we take information in, as people, is via our five senses, meaning that the five senses need to be considered when designing a deliberate Customer Experience. All of these are measured intuitively, by each individual. The big change we have made in this definition is by introducing the conscious and the subconscious aspects of a Customer

Experience. This is probably our biggest learning from the past two or three years. We have discovered there is a conscious and a subconscious aspect of every Customer Experience.

In the next chapter, we will go into these in much greater depth, but to give you a flavor, the conscious mind is what you see all around you and you are conscious of. For example as you read this you will be conscious of the words you are reading and their meaning. You will be conscious of how comfortable you are.

The subconscious is all about the signals that are being registered in your subconscious mind but are not reaching your conscious mind. They are being "seen" but do not register in your conscious mind yet. Your conscious mind is not large enough to deal with all the signals it receives, and thus only important messages are received by it.

As you read this, think about whether you are feeling hot, cold, or just right. These signals about how comfortable you are with the temperature were being sent to your subconscious mind, but as they were not important enough to disturb your conscious mind, they remained in your subconscious. If you get too hot or too cold, you reach a threshold where these messages are sent through to your conscious mind and interrupt your thoughts, resulting in a little voice telling you, "Oh, I'm a little cold." You then decide what to do about it.

The same applies with a Customer Experience. There are many signals that organizations give out to customers that tell them what they really think. Our favorite is when you enter a bank, and the pens are on chains. What is the subconscious message this gives to a customer? It says, "We don't trust you."

Here is the critical question for us. Do you know what conscious and subconscious signals you are giving in your experience today? If not, how can you describe your Customer Experience as deliberate? Another critical question: which parts of your Customer Experience drive or destroy most value? If you don't know the answer to this, how do you target your resources? We shall share with you over the next few chapters how we go about doing this.

We find that most organizations don't know the answer to this question, and therefore they focus on things that are not perceived by customers as improving their experience.

How do we know this? Well, every six months we conduct a survey and then webinar on what we call a "Customer Experience Tracker." This monitors trends in the industry. It surveys over 1,000 people in the United Kingdom and the United States, looking at the state of the Customer Experience as measured by organizations and then by customers. There have been several interesting results. In our most recent survey, released in February 2010, we found considerable conflict

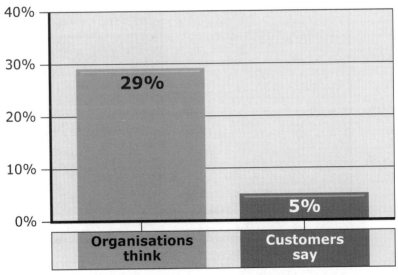

Some action with major improvements

Figure 1.1 How has the customer experience improved over the past six months?

between what organizations think they are doing and how customers perceive it.

For example we asked customers and organizations, "How do you think organizations have improved their Customer Experience in the last six months?" As you will see from Figure 1.1, there is a big gap between what customers and organizations think. Twenty-nine percent of organizations think they have improved their Customer Experience, but only 5 percent of customers would agree! What a disparity! Read another way, this says that 29 percent of organizations are taking action; however, the:

Action being undertaken is the wrong action!

The actions are is clearly not having the desired effect, and customers are not noticing them. At what cost is this happening? Think of the time, money and people that organizations are putting into this with no return.

More worryingly ...

Seventy-one percent of organizations say that they have not improved their Customer Experience.

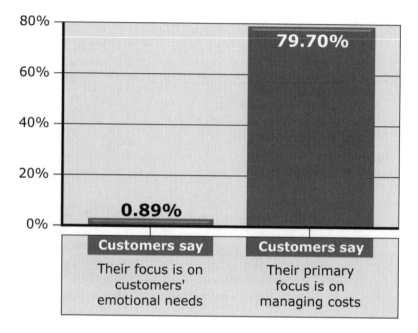

Figure 1.2 When it comes to addressing customers' needs, how do organizations behave?

This is appalling. Nearly three-quarters of organizations are not taking any action to improve their Customer Experience. Most customers, 79 percent, believe all that organizations are worried about are managing costs. We can see from Figure 1.2 that only 0.89 percent of customers think that organizations focus on their emotional needs, therefore:

99 percent of organizations do not focus on customers' emotional needs!

This is a massive opportunity! The challenge is to understand what is required to realize this opportunity. Remember:

Opportunities are never lost; someone will take the one you miss.

(Anon.)

Let us be very clear: someone in your industry will improve their Customer Experience, and using this thinking, it is only a question of who and when. The question you need to ask is, will it be you?

In addition, in our work with academia we have discovered there is a new branch of psychology that had not been looked at before. We are calling it "experience psychology." To understand why customers behave the way they do, it is important to understand experience psychology.

Experience psychology uses criteria to understand customers in much greater depth than the average market research would normally do.

We often get calls from people who say, "We have undertaken research with customers and then implemented work to improve our Customer Experience, but our results are not improving. Why is this?" or "We have been undertaking a Customer Experience program and it has had no effect on our Customer Satisfaction score. Why?" The answer is simple. You do not understand your customers from an experience psychology perspective. The wrong type of research is being carried out, and you are not getting under the skin of your customers, so you are focusing on the wrong things. Here's the irony. These people then say, "Oh, but we know what our customers want," or "We are consumers of our own products, so we know what customers want, as we are customers ourselves." WRONG! You don't know. Your view is tainted by your knowledge. The other push back we get is, "We can't afford to do detailed research." Our reply is to ask them how much time and effort has been wasted on implementing things that don't work. What was the cost of that?

Our view is simple: you must understand the principles of experience psychology to improve any aspect of a Customer Experience.

The second trend we are seeing is the whole area of social media. It's ironic that organizations are making the same mistakes as they always do when a new channel emerges. Typically, their actions follow the following pattern. First, senior managers in the organization try to ignore the opportunity. Second, they make some steps to take advantage of it, but they try to treat the new channel as they do everything else, and after a time, they realize they have made a mistake. Finally, after a good period of time, they put the right investment into developing the new channel. This means they effectively have to unravel the work they have already done, try to salvage the good bits and lose the bad bits. The irony is that if they had considered the issues at the beginning, they would have saved time and money. Isn't it more sensible to realize that social media is going to be a huge channel and embrace it now? That's the way to save time and money.

In working with clients, we have discovered that social media require a new way of thinking. They call for a different mindset. They require a new strategy. All too often we see organizations playing with this. Stop playing and get serious! Social media and its derivatives are going to be enormous! We are talking about a basic human need to socialize and communicate. Granted, social media may morph into something else over the next few years, but the basic human requirement will remain. People are tribal and what to be part of a group, they want to belong, they want to communicate. This is a basic need, and will remain the same whatever the outcome of social media. The words are not important; the behaviors of people –customers – are.

Finally, we shall take a really good look into the future, and look at the fascinating subject of neuroscience: the study of the nervous system, including, most prominently the brain. Don't get put off by its complexity, we have made it simple for everyone to understand.

To retain our thought leadership in the subject of Customer Experience, we have been investigating this for some time, and discussing possibilities of its use in understanding customers with experts on the subject for some time. In fact Qaalfa Dibeehi was a research neuroscientist specializing in computational neuropsychology in a previous work life long ago. Suffice it to say that he knows a bit about the brain.

This is pioneering work. While everyday usable applications for this are some way off, we wanted you to give you a glimpse of the future. This will be a world where you won't have to ask customers questions about what they like; you will be able to read it from their brain activity. Don't get fooled into thinking this is very far away. Companies have already started to redesign their products based on brain scan feedback. There is a growing body of work on the true nature of consumer decision making. Indeed, the first Nobel Prize has already been awarded in this area. It's true we are still in the early stages of applying neuro-science to business, but the tipping point is on this side of the horizon. Remember, people once thought the cellphone was a long way off. Now they are commonplace. We shall expose you to the latest thinking in this area, and explain how we think this will affect you.

Finally, before we get into the meat of the subject matter and onto the next chapter, in this book we are postulating possible, probable, and preferable futures. We are seeking to understand what is likely to change and how it will affect you.

Let's start by looking at experience psychology.

2 Experience psychology: the new field and the end of the marketing Four Ps

It seemed like a good idea at the time and for a while it was a success. Customers flocked to large stores on busy main streets, attracted by value for money and a good location. However, times change and so do consumers. A store environment that was once attractive and engaging became dour, old-fashioned and undesired. Even an affectionately recognized brand could not save the day.

Of course, it only took a change in economic circumstance for Woolworths, a high street general store in the United Kingdom, to go the same way as many other once seemingly impregnable institutions. Rather like the survival of the fittest, what was good for one environment meant extinction in another.

This and other stories seem united by a single theme, one that differentiates the companies that survive and prosper from those that fail. That is the extent to which firms understand and manipulate the Customer Experience they deliver in order to influence consumer choice. If you like, how good are they at being "experience psychologists," designing experiences that stay in the mind, either consciously or subconsciously, as alluring, memorable or engaging – recognizing that in today's world customer relationships are no longer just about the transaction.

In Woolworths' case, the company clearly failed through its inability to appreciate not only what consumers wanted, a very marketing outcome-based concept of product, price, promotion and place, but what consumers perceived the "Woolworths experience" to be. For instance, how they felt walking into a store, what cues and information they used to gain an impression of who Woolworths were, what prejudices and expectations they brought with them – maybe from something they read years ago or heard by word of mouth – even how the experience fitted within their culture? All these are profoundly psychological concepts which were simply missed out in the heavy focus on traditional marketing.

Likewise, if you think about companies that are a success, how an experience is managed and impacts on consumer or client perception has proven all-important; and we are not just talking about the usual suspects, well-known and emotionally engaging brands like Disney and Harley-Davidson. In the case of one of our clients, Overbury, a UK fitting-out and refurbishment business, firmly in the business-to-business sector, the company identified "perfect delivery, on time and on budget" as of key value to its end-client stakeholders, then proceeded to create the perfect delivery experience. In the process it changed its look and feel and way of operating, to revolutionize a previously margin-focused, confrontational business.

Interestingly, it has proven virtually impossible for competitors to recreate the same "experience" even in different shades of "on-budget, on-time" because the whole psychology of "how" it is delivered is fundamental to the organization: it is now not just a marketing concept of we delivered on time and on budget but a feeling and perception of success. Critically, where experience succeeds is when this "how" becomes "what" you desire. In the case of Overbury:

> The key thing is the non-contractual, non-adversarial approach of the staff. They go about their business in a quiet, low-key, confident, manner which the client likes, they're not divisive.
>
> Source: client on-site team

Indeed, it is this people side of the business (the humanic) that now frequently proves the most valuable. For instance, Lorraine Grubbs-West, former Exec VP, Southwest Airlines and author of *Lessons in Loyalty*, tells us how Southwest used their staff to create a "fun" experience for travelers; something which paid dividends when this experience, not the price, became the focus of demand:

> Fun was a core strategy at Southwest Airlines. We pretty much had this strategy to ourselves in the airline industry. Our competitors didn't focus on fun. It wasn't until the early 80s, when, due to fuel prices rising significantly causing every major domestic airline but Southwest to lose money, that our competitors took note and made "fun" their strategy too. However, they didn't take the time to understand what it really was and even less, how to implement it successfully. Many of them forced their employees to go out and have fun with the customer. There is nothing worse than trying to force someone who is not comfortable doing that, so some of them did not do a good job of it.

In increasingly commoditized markets, it is this "experiential side" that is the key differentiator. After all, if the choice between firms on the core product or service demanded is similar, how else will decisions to buy and use again be made? The traditional Four Ps of marketing (price, product, place, and promotion) are simply not enough, and instead we must look beyond the rational to how things feel and are perceived.

In this way, marketing is becoming a psychological discipline; emotion (such as fun in the Southwest Airlines example) and other psychological states take the place of rationality alone.

Indeed within economic theory, the belief that decisions (decision analysis) are made wholly rationally without recourse to the emotions and subconscious is already old hat. In a famous paper, Nobel Prize winner Professor Daniel Kahneman spoke for instance of "bounded rationality": how decision making is impacted by the intuitive and emotional.

Professor Kahneman further makes the key point that:

> the rational model is one in which the beliefs and the desires are supposed to be determined. We were real believers in decision analysis 30 years ago, and now we must admit that decision analysis hasn't held up.[1]

And where economics goes, marketing must surely follow. To illustrate the point, here are the Top Ten examples, in no particular order, of how the psychology of an experience, rather than the items we buy, impacts on its value. These are impacts that go beyond the rational and into the subconscious and emotional (note that this is not a comprehensive list):

1. *We make decisions based on our preconceived expectations of what an experience will be, not what it is.*
    Professor Kahneman (Nobel Prize winner) and Professor Tversky's prospect theory tells us how we notice things based on our benchmark expectations of loss or gain. So paying £10 ($15) extra for sundry items on a budget airline can feel worse than paying £20 ($30) for extras such as sweets, popcorn and hot dogs in a cinema experience!

2. *We don't consider all the elements of an experience, only those most noticeable.*
    In the human mind, decisions are made based on "decision weights" (key aspects of an experience that heavily influence how you decide) rather than probabilities. This is similar to the concept

---

1 Daniel Kahneman: The Thought Leader Interview, Michael Schrage, *strategy+business*, Winter 2003, Issue 33 (www.strategy-business.com/media/file/03409.pdf).]

of cues. An example of this is the power of surprise, whereby one moment can be used as representative of the whole experience because it is most memorable. For instance, we worked with a UK electrical retailer to improve their Customer Experience. Here they created what they called "Father Christmas Moments," where the home delivery driver delivers the television, carefully unwraps it, and polishes it down before leaving. This evokes a feeling that this was a "good experience." Designing in the right "cues" can therefore have a substantial effect on satisfaction.

3. *We identify a moral code in what you do, even if it is not directly relevant to the purchase in question.*
   Developing an experience that shows empathy towards the needs of others is important. The ethical advantage comes from clients' and consumers' perception of your organization as a "moral leader." People trust a brand more than others because of a "giving culture" even though this has no direct relevance to the product or service purchased. For instance, in our work with a leading travel company we found that couples identified with the empathy shown towards families with children even though this was not of relevance to the service purchased.

4. *Sometimes we don't know about the things that influence us, we just subconsciously perceive them.*
   We are often manipulated by things we can hardly recall, like the smell of the bakery in a supermarket, the color of the walls in a hospital, or the tone of voice of the pharmaceutical rep. This has important implications when we think that most Customer Experience is received vicariously, through for instance the one-second visual impressions of a letter, brochure, or advert.

5. *Emotional twinges affect our "in the moment" decision making and hence behavior.*
   With emotion and mood, "gut feel" can affect action. For instance, the mood we are in can moderate our sense of the negative and our openness to the positive; think how music in a supermarket or the use of lighting in a restaurant works intuitively to create the "right mood:"

In 1999 Adrian North, David Hargreaves, and Jennifer McKendrick of the University of Leicester staged a psychology experiment in a wine shop. They found that when French music was played in the shop 77 percent of the wine sold that day was French. When German music was played 73 percent of the wine sold on that day was German. The nationality of the music was changed on alternate days over a two-week period. When questioned after their purchases 86 percent of the customers said categorically that the music did not affect their choice.

www.DerrenBrown.channel4.com

6. *We are prone to be wary of anything that threatens our well-being.*
   As humans we are prone to try to avoid losses more often than we seek gains. Hence, emotionally we will notice the negative more often, and treat the positive as bland or as expected if there is no "wow" or surprise. This is particularly the case in frequently used environments such as a grocery store. Risk management is therefore a key part of your business strategy with implications for the amount of effort you need to put in to service recovery. However there is perhaps more of a worry when the negative is not noticed at all. To quote Mandarin Oriental Hotels:

   You want your customers to feel so possessive and involved in the experience that if you were to change the color of the carpets or the person on the front desk that they would notice and even feel happy to complain.

7. *What we say we want is often not what we "really" want.*
   A customer may say they want a cellphone, but what they really want is a status symbol; a client may say they want a new billing system but what they really want is to further their career by improving their department's productivity and by learning the latest program (for their resumé!). By focusing on the "real demand" not the transaction, we can design a more appealing product or service.

8. *Our memory of an event is not perfect but subject to manipulation.*
   The Peak–End rule (from Professor Kahneman) says that you should focus on managing the peaks of a Customer Experience and its end, as these are most remembered. Ask yourself the question, how much effort is really put into the end of an experience? Do you even know where the end is (or the start, for that matter)? If the answer is very little effort, or that you don't know, then experience psychology is for you.

9. *We like to follow the herd, be seen as part of the group.*
   Even if we don't like to admit it, being part of the group, gaining social status, following a respected leader, is important. Many people like Richard Branson and what he stands for; this has a positive effect on the value of an experience. We will talk much more about being seen as part of the group later in this book as we start to investigate social media.

10. *We get bored with the same old, same old. Sometimes innovation for its own sake is important.*
    Doing the same thing time and time again may seem like a tried and tested formula, but an inability to move with the times can leave you floundering. Keeping pace with fashion, "the way of doing things," is important; unless of course you are being deliberately "retro" and quaint! Sometimes customers don't just want

safety, they want to see novelty. Again you will see examples of this in our chapters on social media.

Clearly, therefore, the psychological foundations of experience are many and varied, and represent a challenging new order.

However, it is also the case that experience psychology can change the nature of the game you are in through its concern with how things are psychologically perceived and manipulated. Ultimately this can lead to finding new ways to differentiate your firm from the competition and expanding your market area. Think about cellphone purchase. It may be the case that at the bottom end of the market you can get the cheapest phone possible, but when it comes down to it, the choice of a cellphone is often not just about price. There is a willingness to pay a premium just for the impression that you can trust the supplier over the long haul; a sense you get from the experience they deliver. It is not something hard and concrete like the price on the box. Instead it is a look and feel issue, a psychological perception of how staff interact with you, maybe even the way a bill is written.

Cerritos Library in the United Sates understands this concept of developing loyalty and a new market space through the use of the entertainment emotions; essentially turning the staid positioning of libraries on its head. The proof of this has been increased demand from US shopping malls for Cerritos Library tenants, because mall managers recognize Cerritos's ability to retain shoppers ,particularly when at least one member of a family would rather be entertained than walk around the stores! Don Buckley of Cerritos Library tell us a bit about the library:

> The library started back in the late 1990s when people thought that libraries were irrelevant due to the Internet. Waynn Pearson had an opportunity to get money for computers but he turned this down, stating he wanted to build the "library of the future." We looked at service outside the library, in particular, the Ritz-Carlton and the doorman, concierge services, staff saying "good morning" as customers enter. We then compared this best practice with the regular library service where no one says hello, you can walk around and no one will greet you or help you. We took these learnings and integrated them into our Wow Customer Service – themeing using Disney and Hollywood advisors as well as a scriptwriter for Quincy.

Of course, the experience psychology angle also means designing a psychologically engaging experience that will appeal to your key consumer segments. Don Buckley continues:

When we imagined the library we thought, what is the hardest group to attract? This was the 12–25 age group, junior high school, pre-teens through colleges, who in most communities were not in the library. What is this group attracted to? Mall structures, where they can see their friends at the escalators. So the library was made to look like a mall. We have escalators, world-class glasswork and an aquarium. Many people say. "Where are the books?" The books are revealed to them as they explore the library. And that's the idea.

We have a 40ft dinosaur with a TV screen in the base that shows how it was excavated, discovered, preserved and brought to Cerritos. So kids can touch it. There is a learning centre next door.

And what applies to consumers equally applies to business-to-business clients, where it is never just about price specified at tender, but also about perceptions of how the relationship between supplier and client will unfold over the life of a project.

In this context we often see how human psychology trumps market psychology. As an example, consider the BBC program *Dragon's Den*, where inventors pitch products and services for venture capital funding. If we took a non-experience view we might expect that any decision on whether to back a proposal would be made purely on financial grounds. In fact, while having the numbers stack up is clearly important, what is equally of concern are the questions, "As an investor can I do business with this person?," "Can I trust them in the long term?" "Do I like them?" and "Does their pitch persuade me and provide confidence in them as a potential business partner?"

How a firm presents itself becomes more important than *what* it presents. In other words the experience of doing business with the firm, and how that reflects on any perceptions of risk, is perhaps more fundamental than marginal price differences.

This business-to-business experience advantage has also been highlighted by Professor Hugh Wilson of Cranfield School of Management in the United Kingdom:

A senior executive in the air travel industry relayed how a billion dollar order had been placed with a more expensive supplier on the strength of some strong advocacy by another customer. The supplier, they said, had "dug us out of a hole" when aircraft had been expensively grounded through no fault of the supplier, throwing substantial resources fast at getting the planes back in the air and saying that issues of negotiating payment could wait until the crisis was solved.

If Customer Experience Management, then, is concerned with seeing the world through the customer's eyes, thinking as they think and feeling as they feel, in order to understand what an experience truly means, experience psychology brings this to life by making real the "mind of the consumer" as it engages in an experience.

In this book we shall discuss how experience psychology can help your business find differential value in this new order, based as it is more on what happens, and less on the offer itself – in other words "making something the same, feel like something different."

So what is experience psychology?

When we look at experience as a "psychology" we can start to see that experience actually represents any meaningful information received by customers about your firm. For instance, think how some of the most poignant things we can say about a company come from snippets of information that are often years out of date. Imagine the damage being done to corporate reputation amongst the banking sector today! Also with the massive speed of the Web and the connections through social media, a poor experience is talked about faster than ever before.

In this way what really matters psychologically is not the actuality of an experience, but how an experience is perceived!

Experience psychology, then, is about how psychological theory and practice can be used to improve a customer's perception of your experience. By improvement, we mean a focus on the value derived from the emotional and the subconscious experience, not just the rational; an approach that fits psychologically with how we perceive things. To quote Dr Peter Jones of Shire Professional Chartered Psychologists:

> One figure which always surprises people is that the subconscious processes 200,000 times more information than the conscious mind without us having to focus on it, and does that processing before our eyes have even recognized the person or object. It is disposed to process emotions even faster, around ten times faster than our conscious mind.

In practical terms, this relates to emotional and subconscious design, a juicer by Philippe Starck (a famous French product designer), or the design of a Cerritos Library. Alternatively, for a service it means the tone of voice of the operator, the friendliness of the sales rep, or the clarity of a bill. Billing is more important than you might think, considering that we have little to do with a utility unless something goes wrong.

Emotional and mood design clearly and straightforwardly evoke a felt or aesthetic response. Subconscious design, while not mutually exclusive from emotion, has a beneath-the-conscious-surface impact

16

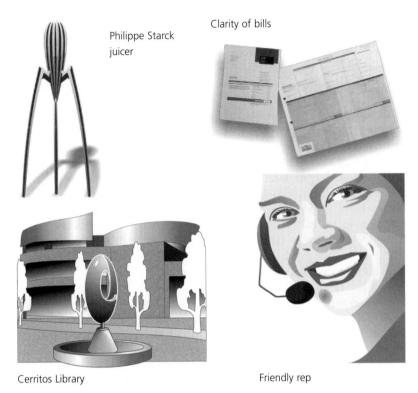

Philippe Starck
juicer

Clarity of bills

Cerritos Library

Friendly rep

Figure 2.1 Emotional and subconscious design

that we would have difficulty expressing if we were asked "What was so good about that experience?" We just know it was!

> Here the juicer and the library are emotionally engaging, the clarity of the bill and the professional tone of voice subconsciously so. And while there is an expectation of functional excellence, the emphasis is in fact less on the juicer's pulping capability, the library's stock of books, the low price of a phone bill or the fastest capability to send out a subcontractor, and more on this "emotional-subconscious" psychological impact of the experience.

To further illustrate the experience psychology approach, we shall now take a journey through the mind of the consumer as it interacts with an experience (the mind journey) before outlining in the next section some of the experience psychological research techniques that can help us understand the impact of the subconscious and emotional. (This is our Future Trend #1.) Then in Chapter 4 we shall look at the impact of group psychology on the experience (our Future Trend #2).

The mind journey

Experience psychology is about changing the experience you offer "as it is perceived in the mind of the consumer" to evoke a valuable effect. The experience argument is that Woolworths failed not so much because of its pricing or products, but because of how it came across.

But of course, to understand the "how to" depends also on understanding the "how is." In other words, how is your Customer Experience perceived today? So imagine you are a customer. What picture can you build of that person's psychology in engaging in an experience?

Traditionally this kind of insight has come from market research and executive intuition. In the future, however, we shall see a more comprehensive psychological profiling approach, which builds on advances in statistical knowledge and consumer understanding. It is the perfect marriage between techniques that seek to represent the whole consumer psyche, and the kind of tools used to model complex physical systems such as the weather or nuclear explosions.

Before we outline these techniques, though, we shall show you how an experience works psychologically. This is very different from how it has been perceived to work before. For instance, instead of focusing on the physical experience alone, the mind journey focuses on the *mindspace experience*, where psychologically the customer is not actually interacting with an experience, but is nonetheless influenced by it, and the *interacting experience*.

The mindspace experience

1. The *pre-experience experience* comprises the psychological baggage consumers bring with them to an experience, which affects what they want to see.
2. *Experiencing intent* comprises what consumers seek from an experience. This marks out the things in an experience that have psychological impact.
3. *Remembering the experience* is concerned with how experience is remembered and socialized; how we "bend" our psychology to fit in with our social group.

Interacting experience

4. *Interacting with the experience* is concerned with how consumers interact with an experience psychologically.

Before we begin, though, a word of warning. We are not seeking to substitute the intuition of executives. On the contrary, by making us better informed, customer psychological profiling is supportive of the "intuitive organization," moving us away from the tied-up-in-knots type of company that suffers from an overdose of "measurementisis." One of the lessons of Malcolm Gladwell's book *Blink* is that intuition goes with experience. The more experienced we are, the more intuitive we become, and the better decisions we make.

Mindspace experience

The pre-experience experience

Definition: here psychologically the client or consumer is implicitly involved. In other words they are not really thinking about you at all, instead they are soaking up impressions of you like a sponge from the messages they receive. Here we look at consumers' psychological relationship with you on the basis of:

- *the prejudices they hold about you*
- *the expectations they have about you*
- *the associations they have built about you.*

Principle 1: Understand prevailing prejudice

There is a famous experiment conducted by Hastorf and Cantril[2] which demonstrates how prevailing prejudice can seriously manipulate the facts. This relates to a particularly rough game of American Football that took place between Dartmouth and Princeton colleges in November 1951. After the match each side blamed the other for the game having become so rough. Taking this as a cue for a psychology experiment, the two researchers were able to replay movie footage of the whole game to students from each college. Yet even in this scenario the same result was obtained: both thought that the rough game was the other side's fault. Although clearly both sides were watching the same game, the reality is that it was perceived differently by the two competitors.

As in sport, so in business. The prevailing prejudice towards, for instance, an overseas call center can seriously damage goodwill. Imagine that a staff member from the storecard handling unit at Marks & Spencer, a highly respected retailer in the United Kingdom, or Macy's, the US store chain, phones a customer to check on a suspected fraud on their account. This is in itself an excellent gesture, designed to ensure

---

2 1954, quoted in Plous, S (1993) *The Psychology of Judgement and Decision-Making*, New York: McGraw-Hill.

that the customer does not lose money because of a fraud they might not yet have noticed. But if the customer assumes they are calling from an overseas call center, this might affect how the call is perceived. At the worst, the customer might not perceive the good intention at all, but simply wonder, "Is this a scam?"

In much the same way we can also see how old media reports can still influence a consumer's perception of an experience many years after the event. For instance, in our work in the utility sector, the issue of water leaks came up time and again as indicative of how wasteful and pricey utilities are, even though media reports of water leaks were long past.

Of course a positive prevailing prejudice can help enormously; it leads customers to put a positive light on their experiences, which is particularly useful when things go wrong. If a well-regarded company like Apple or Nordstrom makes a mistake, customers will tend to think that it's just one of those things, that they were unlucky. But if they have a problem with a brand that they have a less positive perception of, they will not be so generous. You will always be up against it if there is a prejudice against your firm or your industry. But of course therein lies the opportunity, as Overbury found out. They managed to turn their Customer Experience in what is typically a confrontational business, the construction industry, into an "on-time, to budget" perfect delivery experience.

The point here is that all organizations need to be aware of the emotional and subconscious impact of customers' prejudices on their ongoing perceptions and expectations. Clients and customers are not wholly rational; they will be guided in their behavior by these feelings.

Principle 2: Understand expectations

What we expect from an experience is key to how we judge it. Think about the wait time in a doctor's surgery. In Britain at least, people expect a long wait time to see their doctor, and since they expect it, they find the wait less aggravating than a similar wait time in a retail bank. Likewise, people tend to expect a far higher level of profession-alism and friendliness from cast members working at Disneyland than from the local PC outlet, so living up to its brand promise is harder for Disneyland. Even when we have never experienced an event before, we will usually be able to imagine it, and this gives us an expectation of what will occur.

To change expectations is both a tremendous opportunity and a threat. If you reduce customer and client expectations, you risk losing your value differentiator. Take the example of no-frills airlines. In the short run it is true that a reduced price can attract but where is the value differentiator, if at the end of the day what you are offering is pretty much the same as the next provider?

The lesson from expectations is that you lose your value differentiators at your peril. This is something anyone involved in cost efficiency exercises around Six Sigma/Lean or any other business process re-engineering initiative should be aware of and prepared to audit.

Principle 3: Experience as association

It is well known that the brain is made up of a network of neural connections. What we think and feel about anything is intimately connected to other relevant experiences. This is why so much of our relationship with a product or service is not just about what happens when we interact with it physically today, but also about the associations created in the mind over time.

For instance, what is the first thing that comes to mind when a client or consumer hears mention of your company? Do you think it is the product or service you sell, or something else? The truth is that for all companies, what they sell is just the starting point. Coke is more than just a fizzy drink: why else would it outsell Pepsi, even though in blind tastings people prefer Pepsi? IBM is more than just a product; it used to be said that "no one got fired for buying IBM," and that sense of reassurance is part of what it sells. Even when a company is entirely new to a market, the way it conveys its message and the associations it makes will say something to customers about what to expect.

Rather like the new guy at the party, a brand can be a wallflower, the life and soul of the party, or a me-too player.

Fortunately, however, these mental associations with brands are not fixed forever, but can be manipulated to create an entirely new market. Consider, for instance, how cheese has been repackaged for the children's market as "cheese strings," with suitably engaging characters on each pack. Cheese is now associated with fun in children's minds. The simple selection of the pack to open becomes a matter of entertainment. For that audience, when they "think cheese strings," all sorts of entertaining associations come to mind.

However, an even better scenario would be if we could change consumer's associations with the brand without fundamentally altering the actual product or service. Indeed, this is exactly what happened about 25 years ago when Lucozade set about changing customer perceptions. Previously, it had been seen as a drink associated with sickness – "Lucozade aids recovery" – but a marketing campaign worked to turn it into a drink associated with sportiness – "Lucozade replaces lost energy." The effect was dramatic, with UK sales between 1984 and 1989 tripling to £75 million. Same drink, different experience associations!

For today's marketeer, it is critical to create these positive associations that dominate the "mindspace" – the experience customers have with a firm before and after they touch it.

Unfortunately this can also be a challenge. Perceptions tend to stick around, as was mentioned above. A lot of the associations people have with brands, especially when they are not in a "thinking mode" but are buying reflexively, are difficult to budge. Those memories of past news stories or long-ago advertising campaigns, or even past personal experiences, tend to be resonant, especially if the product or service is one that customers touch upon only intermittently.

Example business implication: manage your one-second moments

But that is not the end of the story, for there is also the power of unseen associations, those subconscious expressions of an experience that color consumer impressions of you. Rather like the power-dressing fashions of the 1980s, a look can speak a thousand words. Perhaps the best expression of this is the "one-second moment." This concerns how a brand's visual portrayal in promotional literature sets the tone of an experience, "locking in" certain associations. For instance, a major utility found that the bill was a heavy influence on consumer experience. In particular, what mattered was how the visual expression of price was communicated; something mortgage companies achieve successfully in their price comparisons, but utility companies fail at because they have a bill layout that customers associate with confusion.

These *one-second moments* are central to understanding associations. In essence they influence consumers at the subconscious level. Why? Because most consumers don't actually care that much about most companies, and when they do have cause to think about a company, these impressions are the ones most resonant in their minds.

Unfortunately, subconscious drivers to value are little understood by many organizations. Yet for us, understanding this instant effect can be a key missing ingredient in much of business research today. To quote from psychology (see psychology.wikia. com/wiki) these one-second moments are akin to the "affect heuristic":

Affect heuristics have yielded startling results. First, the phenomenon can be rapid. Winkielman, Zajonc, and Schwarz flashed one of three images in the view of test subjects: a smiling face, a frowning face, or a neutral geometric shape. The subject was then shown a Chinese ideograph and asked how he or she liked it. The test subjects preferred the ideographs they saw after the smiling face, even though the smiling face was shown only for 1/250 of a second, and the subject did not recall seeing it.

Using an area of psychology called IAT (Implicit Association Test), this kind of instant association can be mapped as a network of links. These links represent visual impressions or key words of your experience. This is akin to the Freudian word association test – you say mother, I say father – where speed of response to a word or picture is used to test a person's gut reaction. This map of associations is rather like neuron linkages in the brain. The key point is that these one-second moments are subconscious, not rationally based effects, used by consumers to judge you – whether to buy or not to buy, and so forth. In most cases they are in fact the main experience consumers will have of you before they interact with you. They are critical customer experiences.

Experiencing intent

Definition: here psychologically the client or consumer is more involved, thinking about engaging with you and more focused on their involvement with you. Here we look at the consumer's psychological relationship with you on the basis of:

■ *how successful they feel you are at understanding their well-being.*

Principle 4: Understand well-being

In "traditional" marketing terms, well-being is about "what I seek from engaging with your company" – maybe a cheaper price or a quality product. In experience psychology terms, though, it is not quite as simple as that. Well-being is also about the journey and the use. For instance, this can be about the attitude of the delivery man for your washing machine, the sense of 1990s design on the Eurostar (the train service that runs between the United Kingdom and France/Belgium) or the confusing text on your electricity and gas bill. Sure, a customer might think, I didn't buy your product with these in mind, but they most certainly affect my well-being.

Understanding your value-in-use

Indeed it is because of this that academics have recently started to talk about value-in-use – the value derived not just from what is sought, but also from how a product or service performs. To quote from Professor Hugh Wilson:

> Value-in-use is not gained at the moment when the supplier delivers a product or service – the moment which is assessed in most event satisfaction surveys – but as a result of the customer's consumption processes when they use the product or service. An MBA is used in job interviews or in applying the knowledge gained to the development of a strategic plan. An aircraft engine is used to keep a plane in the air. A customer relationship management system is used to improve retention, or reduce cost to serve, or improve share of wallet.

Value-in-use is perhaps one of the key marketing ideas of the last few years. To illustrate the point, if we think about a mining project, what we might demand is the right-sized hole. This is the functional outcome. What we are less bothered about is the size of the drill-bit, in other words the functional attribute. Yet this is exactly what most firms end up selling. Walk into any cellphone store, and the focus is on functionality, with little emphasis on "how" a product is used and hence "what" functional outcomes are or could be required. For example, perhaps there is a focus on reliability and ruggedness for business users or design for the teenage market. Even if there is, this lacks reflection in store layout, merchandising, promotion and sales talk.

My well-being is neglected!

This is an endemic effect, and something we will come to in our later chapters on social media, but in short it appears that firms are sometimes more worried about the technology than the use, *why* people are using their product!

In our work, however, we take this one stage further. Value is also derived from the whole psychological impact of the experience. For instance, how the experience is expressed is important: the appearance, not just the function. This can be as specific as the appearance of staff onsite or the way a process chart is laid out. Leading companies, for instance, clearly understand the value potential of ensuring that even the simplest interactions with customers or suppliers are recognized as important.

Of course it is also important to bear in mind that what is good for one group is not necessarily good for another. Emotionally different consumer segments will be influenced in different ways by the same experience. Think of a football match: it's the same match but person A, a supporter of the winning side, acts with joy at the result, whereas person B, who doesn't actually care that much and only came along for the hot dogs, reacts with indifference.

In our Moment Mapping® service we help companies design and build emotionally engaging experiences that define the moments of contact, the journey through which your various customer groups pass when they do business with you.

Example business implication: understand your client and consumer goals

Achieving well-being is about the goals we seek, which in turn define our emotional and motivational state. Mapping these out, however, is not as easy as it sounds, for goals operate at various levels. Take a simple shopping trip to get the weekly groceries. There are high-level goals, the strategic achievement of getting the right goods at the right price. Then there are the lower-level tactical goals which may or may not impact on the higher-level goals, from "I couldn't find a place to park" (distress, strategic goal subverted) through to "This queue is a bit longer than I expected" (mild aggravation, tactical goal not achieved).

Goal mapping is something we turn to in later chapters, where we show you just how to do it.

Remembering the experience

Definition: here the client or consumer is socializing and rationalizing the memory of the experience into learning. This is taken forward and used to influence future decisions. At this stage, the influence of the group can be quite important, as are stereotypes which form in the mind as the memory becomes more concrete. Here we look at the consumers' psychological relationship with you on the basis of:

■ *how well you understand their memory of an experience*
■ *how well you understand how memories are socialized.*

Principle 5: Understand memory

How memory works essentially dictates who you are. It is no good building a fantastic experience if all that's remembered is what went wrong. Who would for instance remember the great Harland & Wolff shipyards other than as the place where the *Titanic* was built? Ultimately as what is remembered is what is real, the corporate focus should be on communicating the right cues and building the correct level of emotional engagement into an experience to make it memorable.

Maxine Clark, Founder, Chairman and Chief Executive Bear of Build-A-Bear Workshop®, for instance, follows this principle by making the whole experience a personal and thereby memorable one:

> Our mission states that we want it to be fun for our guests; fun for us and that we connect with guests' emotions depending on who it is and who is coming into our store. For instance, someone might be wanting to make a bear for a child that was just born, a young man might be making a bear to ask a young lady to marry him, somebody might be making a dog because their dog has recently passed away, they had a black lab and they want to make a black lab so that they will always have that dog. There are so many emotions, happy and sad, that people go through, and our stores help them steer, and I think the number one thing that we hope it will always be is a wonderful memory and a fun experience.

For memory also read memorabilia, for if we follow the Peak–End rule – that what we remember most are the peaks of an experience and the end – then creating a memorable end can impact on how we feel afterwards. It is just unfortunate that ends are typically neglected, as are many peak moments such as service recovery, which represents a real opportunity to embed some positive psychology.

Principle 6: Understand socialization trends

This is closely allied to the memory of an experience and how these memories become socialized. We may for instance "in the moment" view the selection of a restaurant, a pair of shoes or the purchase of a new computer system as a close-run thing between competing alternatives. However, after purchase and through talking to others our decision becomes socialized and concrete. It was always going to be the case!

Embedding cues to justify a decision is in fact one of the key trends we see in many businesses today as they move from a focus on brand to a focus on group psychology. Starbucks is a classic example of this, how buying a coffee has social cachet around environmentalism. Likewise with other ethical concepts such as the Red Card (a charge card that pays a proportion of turnover to charity), making the customer or client feel they are part of a social trend rather than an outsider.

Example business implication: manage your group psychology

If past marketing has been about the individual's relationship with an experience through the brand halo, future marketing is about managing group psychology. Look at how Harley-Davidson has gone beyond the brand to build just such a group feeling. Thinking about who your customers are and their psychology as a group has also been of significance in the Cerritos experience design. We look at group psychology in a later chapter of this book.

Interacting experience

In this section we have moved away from the mindspace experience and now start interacting with the "real" experience.

Experience psychology: interacting with the experience

Now the customer or client is physically interacting with an experience, primed by prejudice, expectation and desired goals. This is where what you actually do has an impact. Here we look at the consumer's psychological relationship with you on the basis of:

- *how well you understand how heuristics work*
- *how well you understand "subconscious value"*
- *how well you understand mood effects.*

Principle 7: Understand heuristics

A heuristic is a rule of thumb that customers or clients use to make some decision about you. Heuristics are in effect special cases of cues used to make a determination as to the value of a product or service. To illustrate the point, take the case of a large hotel chain that found its customer satisfaction scores always remained the same in one room no matter what action they took. It was only after a member of staff decided to sleep in the room that the answer was found: a small wet patch on the ceiling at eye level. This detail was in effect a cue for lack of cleanliness, no matter how much effort had previously been put into the room.

This can of course also work to your advantage. An inherently poor or bland experience can be enlivened by the simple addition of "fun elements" or wow moments of surprise. This is something that Stew Leonard, a convenience store in the United States, learned when they introduced animatronics into their stores. Likewise, a focus on the human-to-human relationship side, whether this is through tone of voice in a call centre (First Direct, a telephone bank in the United Kingdom), the way staff smile (Southwest Airlines) or the visually professional onsite approach (Overbury), can act to alter perceptions far more than the actual delivery of the product or service.

Another example is Carphone Warehouse, a cellphone store in the United Kingdom, which makes great use of cues. Here, a show is made of determining the correct cellphone for you by logging details into a computer system that delivers details of the top few phones of relevance to your needs.

These cues exist everywhere, and are often critical in the first few seconds of an experience, setting the mood for what to expect. Interestingly, they can also work quite well dissonantly, cutting against the grain of expectation. Consider the launch of Microsoft's Bing.com: with its focus on nature scenes and even slightly quirky format, its ambience is almost Apple-like!

On the negative side it is also important to realize that a noticeably bad experience can also stick in the memory and impact consumer decision making.

Principle 8: Understand subconscious value

How much of customer satisfaction is driven by subconscious experience? That is not an easy question to answer, yet if we accept that there is a subconscious experience, then we must also accept that there is such a thing as subconscious value.

We have already seen for instance the kind of subconscious, "below the waterline" effect of one-second moments, visual impressions and the power of surprise. Yet there are other aspects of an experience – maybe the ease of filling out a booking form, or the acceptability of a credit card in-store – that are often titled "hygienic," and are value-critical at a subconscious level.

In many ways we can view the subconscious in the same way as a magician's sleight of hand. Subtle and unseen changes can evoke a strong reaction. And what is true of the mundane is also true of the more deliberately designed elements of an experience. Disney, for instance, understands this, designing in subconsciously perceived value. The super-clean streets not only lead to a positive environment but also discourage further littering.

This kind of response is not just confined to the more experience-oriented services. It has long been known, for instance, that music has an impact on the subconscious, affecting our mood, our inclination to buy, and our length of store browse time. It is worth mentioning as well that silence can also affect an experience, although often more insidiously, leading to feelings of isolation.

Too often, though, analysis of decision making is post hoc without recourse to in-the-moment effects that so often demonstrate the impact of the emotions and an immediate, fleeting subconscious. Yet it is these emotional twinges that tell us as consumers and clients the path to follow. For instance, how many times have you made a decision to go to restaurant A over B, because you felt like it that day? And what images are brought to mind at the point at which that decision is made?

In truth decisions are made with significant reference to how we feel at a subconscious level. Your consumer and client profile must therefore take account of not only what customers say influences their decision making, but also those things that they do not report.

Principle 9: Understand mood

Mood is a much under-rated but important ingredient of an experience. In many ways it is also the most mysterious, for mood has little to do directly with your goals in experiencing something. Instead it is a diffuse and long-lasting reaction to an environment.

Whether this is by lighting effects in a restaurant or music in a store, how you use mood is important, because if all else fails, this remains within your control. Indeed a number of academic studies have shown that if you put consumers in a positive frame of mind they are more likely to forgive your errors and applaud your successes. Mood is, if you like, the great moderator, reducing the impact of the negative and encouraging the positive.

Example business implication: understand your experience's heart-rate

One interesting way to demonstrate the effect of mood is through the use of a heartbeat monitor. Here we looked at a journey by train from Milton Keynes to Holyhead, in the United Kingdom. This used our Moment Mapping service® but with a twist. Instead of relying just on verbal reports we also sought to measure stress points via a heartbeat monitor. The peak moments!

What was most noticeable about this was the reduction in relative stress levels at point A (see below) which happened to coincide with the more relaxing "countryside effect." Same train journey, different mood.

The point is that this effect would have not been captured too well without some subconscious/emotional measure. Indeed when we have used the same technique across other experiences we have been able to see how restaurant environments fail to evoke the same levels of relaxation as a home environment, or how anticipation of an event leads to falls and rises in stress rates, not just during the event itself but before it happens too!

In experience design, this is crucial. Design for anticipation and understand where relaxation really becomes memorable.

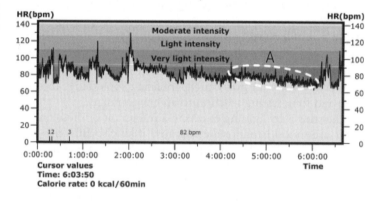

Figure 2.2 Touchpoint mapping by heartbeat

In this chapter we learned about the new field of experience psychology, and how your clients and consumers not only interact physically with you, but also go through a psychological journey with you: the mindspace experience. In the next chapter we show you the tools and techniques you can use to understand how experience psychology can work for you.

3 Experience psychology research

Business research is a little bit like "the tail wagging the dog." Because it's easy to measure the rational, conscious side of an experience through customer satisfaction surveys and the like, it must therefore be true that people do indeed make decisions rationally. Yet, no matter how hard researchers try, eventually even they must admit that rationality alone fails to predict adequately how people actually behave.

It's like we understand the tip of the iceberg but not below the waterline – where incidentally the biggest impacts on client and consumer decision making are felt.

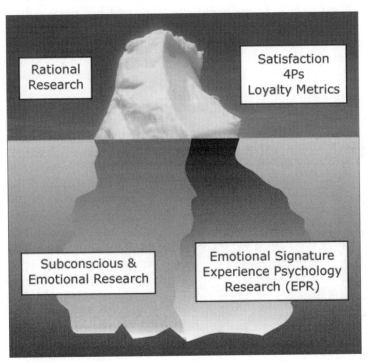

Figure 3.1 The iceberg of impacts on customer decision making

For us, then, it seems as if there is something fundamental missing: that something being a way to measure how people feel about an experience, not just how they rationalize it.

To illustrate the point, think about how we make any decision as clients and consumers to *buy* or *not to buy*, to *browse* or *not to browse*. Quite naturally and obviously this is "in the moment" using both our thoughts and our feelings; even high-value items that seemingly require a lot of thought, such as buying a car, ultimately come down to a decision moment colored not just by rationality but also by how we feel. Yet so much of research simply fails to capture this critical "in-the-moment" effect; it's quite a step to say that the decision-making process in a focus group is the same as what happens in real life, or even that a customer can recreate all the influences that led to a previous decision.

Hence, if you ask a customer three months later why they bought that car, of course their answer will be all about the price and product features, when in fact it was these things and more that actually caused them to choose it. Perhaps they were heavily influenced by the rep being really nice to them, their partner's encouragement in the showroom, or simply the way the car was presented, how it just kind of spoke to them!

All the analysis in the world after the event will never quite take you back to that moment, when your customer was sitting in the car, imagining themselves driving it. Perhaps at the end of the day it was the cup-holder in the car, the smell of the leather seats, the many subconscious fleeting impulses felt and remembered that did it for them.

So are we really getting accurate results by asking for such feedback outside the event, or are we just getting feedback? If you ask a customer a question, they'll give you an answer that sounds rational, because they are thinking, "I'd hate to say, you know, I really bought that car because I fell for the sales rep's patter."

Clearly then, you

Figure 3.2 Choosing to buy a new car

should be finding ways to incorporate emotional and intuitive measures into your research, even if this might seem a little difficult. In addition, you should also take a consultancy approach to your research, for without that expert eye data can be misinterpreted, statistics being as much an art as a science. And finally you must consider your method. After all, would you buy a house from a bunch of cowboy builders without any skill in house construction? In the same way, ask yourself the question, is your research trustworthy?

Research is almost like the *Trojan horse* of business. Because you can always get an answer, it is easy to use and abuse as a political tool. This is why our experience psychology methods are complex but clearly communicated, methodologically rigorous, and led by experienced consultants who act as Sherpas climbing with you up the mountain of Customer Experience metrics.

Let us then take you up the mountain and show you some of the key techniques we feel will enable you to move your Customer Experience away from measuring "just rationality" into measuring the emotional and the subconscious; to turn your customer research into experience psychology research.

To help us along the way we will use some principles from psychological research. For instance, we use the analogy of an onion. When you think about it, an onion has many layers, and so too with consumer response. You need to peel back the onion, get behind the meaning of a need or want, to get at the true root cause.

Consider this: when someone asks you "How are you today?" how do you answer? If you are having a bad day, do you say, "I'm glad you asked, I'm feeling a little depressed today." Of course you don't. The normal response to the question is "Yes, I'm fine." This reply shows the outer skin of the onion. The same applies with customers. How many times have you been at a restaurant when the waiter comes around and asks "Is everything all right?" Do you always tell them the truth? Maybe the food is a little cold, or the steak is not exactly as you like it. Often people think "It's not worth the hassle of explaining what I don't like," or "I feel embarrassed saying that the food is a little cold. It's actually not bad, so I won't say anything." People do not necessarily say what they truly feel for many reasons. Therefore, it is important to peel back the onion of customer response: to get behind what people say and understand what they don't say!

Preparing to climb: a map and a compass

In preparation for our journey, we have already described the mind journey: the pre-experience experience, experiencing intent, remembering the experience, and interacting with the experience. This is akin to our journey map. But what else should we take along in our rucksacks? If we exclude the obvious fundamentals like food, clothing, and camping equipment, what guidance tools do we need? A compass, a walkie-talkie of course, and more – which means in Customer Experience metric terms experience psychology research tools. The first of these that we will look at is the Emotional Signature®.

Emotional Signature® – the mind journey compass

Clearly as your Sherpa we cannot do without a compass, and so too with Customer Experience metrics – we need a methodology to give us clear direction as to where we are heading. This is the Emotional Signature®, the subject of our book *The DNA of Customer Experience: How emotions drive and destroy value.*

In this book and following two years of research vetted by Professor Voss of the London Business School, we discovered the emotions that drive and destroy value. Before finding out what these are, though, try this experiment without looking at Figure 3.3 overleaf. Take a piece of paper and write down the 20 emotions you think drive and destroy value, taking care to say which ones drive and destroy the most value.

Bearing in mind that there are hundreds of possible emotion terms, we suspect you did not find that such an easy task.

From our research, however, the answer becomes obvious. You will see in Figure 3.3 that the 20 emotions our research has identified are broken into four clusters: negative emotions that destroy value; attention emotions such as *interested* which make something feel appealing; recommendation emotions, which are all about the touchy-feely side of the experience; and advocacy emotions, which together are close to the concept of total satisfaction.

Perhaps you chose some of the advocacy and destroying emotions in Figure 3.3. An obvious one people usually include is the concept of feeling satisfied. Notice how in Emotional Signature® however we talk about dissatisfaction, but not satisfaction. We suspect, though, that many readers will not have chosen many of the attention and recommendation emotions we identified.

As a diagnostic tool, then, Emotional Signature® acts in a way like your customer satisfaction survey, the difference being that now we are measuring not just rational response over a few items, but the rational, the emotional, and the subconscious across the holistics of an experience.

In this way we are modeling a complete view of the customer or client

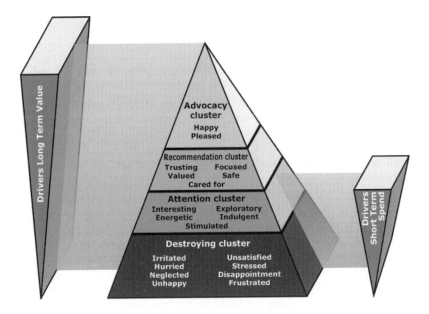

Figure 3.3 The hierarchy of emotional value

psyche. Indeed, we go through an example of how we applied Emotional Signature® to social media in further chapters of this book.

Emotional Signature® does not stop there, though, for we still need to put some solid numbers behind the answer to how much value we can get by focusing on an emotionally engaging experience. This is not an easy thing. To make this compass work requires expert skills in statistics, predictive modeling, emotion theory, theories of implicit response, and ideally a strong dose of Customer Experience expertise, along with expert communication. So it is quite a brew! Yet without getting into its complexities, it should be useful for us to describe a few of the fundamentals to you.

In Emotional Signature® we have a simple structure:

1 *There is a stimulus* – the Customer Experience, whether this is about the comfort of a chair or the tone of voice of a call centre agent.
2 *There is a response* – the subconscious, the emotional, and the rational impact of experiencing these stimuli.
3 *There is an effect.* This is the valued outcome your business seeks through engaging with a client or customer. It could be about

increasing levels of spend, tenure, or attitude: for instance customer satisfaction, recommendation, or trust.

What we are trying to do is to see how much value we can predictably get by changing the stimuli (which we hope to control) in a certain way: stimuli that run the whole gamut of an experience, not just four or five items. For instance, how much value can we get by changing items that are sometimes ill-considered in research, such as the color of the carpet or the tone of voice of the call center rep? All these are seen and measured through the lens of the rational, emotional, and subconscious.

Of course this sounds complex, and it *is* complex, but for us this is rather like building a bridge. Most decision makers don't want to be troubled with seeing the detailed blueprints, but they do want to be inspired by the output, which in our case means that they want to be comfortable that we are producing the best data possible for decision making. So the modeling is complex but the result is simple, actionable, empirical, and highly robust. And of course the "secret source" in all this is how we build in the emotions and the subconscious. Miss this out and you cannot trust your results: they are literally half-baked!

Just as a brief taster, here are five things we have found from this research:

First, there is an emotional and a subconscious experience that drives and destroys value, one that you can definitely quantify.

Second, we can identify what elements of your physical experience these emotion effects relate to, which of course answers the "So what do we do about it?" question.

Third, we can identify an "experience gap," the difference between what you do today and what people actually want. This is quite critical. Most of research fails miserably to address this. To illustrate the point, let's go back to our buying a car example:

A customer buys a car from the only garage in town. They would like to be able to choose from a greater variety of cars, but only a few types are on offer. They decide to go with the cheapest. So a cheap price does drive their spend, but to accurately model their psychology we need also to think about their future desires.

In short, just because something does not exist in your experience today does not mean people don't want it! In Emotional Signature® we research what people want, not just what is on offer!

Fourth, we have found through our database the unique "Emotional Signatures" of various industry groups and segments of consumers and clients. both B2B and B2C. This is a useful point of comparison that answers the question, we all do the same thing physically but do we feel different?

Fifth, we have found that in doing this work you have to accept a significant mind shift that affects all your research to date. You need to accept that what is important is not the "physical thing" (the stimulus), but the "physical interaction" among things: what it means to me!

Ultimately, it is this interaction that better represents customer perception, and Customer Experience is all about the reality of things "as perceived" in the consumer's mind.

This is admittedly a difficult point, so let us explain by example:

> Maybe you go to a Mexican restaurant with low expectations, but actually get an excellent meal. Now you start to become attuned to the experience. The quality of the food is something that no longer acts in isolation to raise your level of satisfaction, but also starts to have an effect on other aspects of the experience. You start to notice how good the décor is; perhaps you even notice negative things, like the waiter's poor customer service, and how you wish they played authentic Mexican folk music.

We can now see from this example what this mind shift means. While food quality here is critical, it does not act alone; it impacts other things, and it is this interaction that changes value.

To illustrate the point further, we once got the following question from a travel client operating under tough margins. If we were to remove or change a small part of their Customer Experience (in this case information boards) what would be the effect on the value they offered to customers? Or to put it another way, what was the value of the information boards in hard cash terms?

The answer was zero. Why, you might ask? It was because the client was asking the wrong question. The real question they needed to ask was, "What is the value of the information-getting experience?" In other words, customers have a desire to obtain information. They need that information, and they have an experience in the process of getting it. We therefore need to measure their perception of achieving this goal, not the value of the concrete physical item. The customer's goal is "Let's find out the information," never "Let's find the information board."

However, asking about the perception of things means that we need to define a complex of stimuli that are bundled together, just as in the Mexican restaurant example, to drive or destroy value. And this is the key point: we want to understand these bundles, in such a way that we can get to a clear priority order of actions.

Emotional Signature® is the key measurement tool needed by businesses and organizations today to fully appreciate the psychology of their experience and how to redesign it for greater value. It is the Customer Experience metric, and for us as Sherpas this is where we frequently begin with clients.

But of course things don't end there. Emotional Signature® lets us measure all sorts of different routes up our mountain. For instance, it lets us undertake emotional segmentation: in other words, we can now consider how emotions differ between different customer groups. We can look for alternative routes to generate value.

In a construction services company we found, for instance, that emotionally the experience was end-client based but with significant detractors in the service for intermediaries like architects, quantity surveyors, and project managers, yet it was this group that advised on where the next projects would be coming from.

Likewise, in our work with a transport company we defined a significant emotional difference between different traveler groups, with the core segment that was driving most value being inconsistent with the segment the company actually wanted to target!

Looking at segments through the lens of emotion can come up with different ways to approach your customer or client base, which you might not have thought about by considering the rational alone. For instance, how different are your high recommenders (in net promoter terms, your promoters) from your low recommenders (your detractors)?

Likewise, when we want to give advice on the quickest way up a mountain, laying out a clear route on the map, Emotional Signature® helps us do just that. So taking emotion as our goal, our route if you like, we look to Emotional Signature® to guide us in an experience redesign.

For instance, consider how in designing football stadia, a sense of anticipation is built into the design; in churches there is a sense of awe, and in restaurants (at least, some restaurants), a sense of calm. Understanding your emotional drivers is therefore an essential step in the creation of the right experience design. If your company is a bank, for instance, the signature might be based around trust; for a car manufacturer, it could be based on luxury.

To design for emotion our process is thus:

1 Decide on your emotional experience using Emotional Signature®.
2 Hold a workshop and develop five or so scenarios around creating the key emotions.

This is a creative exercise, to storyboard possible new scenarios using the five or so stimuli or bundles you have defined as giving your customers emotional value. In this approach, then, we work up a kind of film script of the new experience – stories are great ways in which we learn lessons and visualize possibilities. Some directors working on new films use storyboards, and in staging experiences they should be used as well!

In addition we can also Moment Map® the experience, getting employee buy-in at the same time as many great ideas.

3   Quantify the predicted outcome of these new scenarios.

Take these five or so scenarios and get customers to comment on, or rate, them. We can use these scores to build models that tell you how much value you can create by a new experience design.

4   Pilot the new design and measure through Emotional Signature® the emotional response.

Steven Walden says, "Look forward in your research, rather than backwards, to define what could be! Research should not just be about predicting the future from the past, but about creating the future from the present."

Preparing to climb: geophys

So now we have a map and a compass, but that is far from all we need to navigate up the mountain. Having a compass is all very well, but that will not help us if buried beneath the snow there are crevasses or obstacles we don't know about. To get round these obstacles we need something that can pick up changes beneath our feet. We need a geophysical map of the surroundings: in much the same way, the customer or client may have a sense of your company from things that sometimes they themselves cannot easily articulate.

Subconscious research – the mind journey geophys

The mind journey geophys relates to how we understand the subconscious mind of the client or consumer. But what does the subconscious mind actually refer to, and can we measure its impact on decision making?

Anecdotally, the famous British "illusionist" Derren Brown has shown the effect that the subconscious mind has on our decisions: in this case he calls them "things we perceive without being aware of them." Taking a member of the public around Hamleys (a famous toy store in London), he correctly predicted that she would buy a giraffe toy and name it "Frank." How did he manage this? It was very simple. The store was dressed up with giraffe-like color patterns, and Brown and others made oblique references to giraffes in speaking to the woman. Importantly, she took all of this in without being aware of it, and it influenced her decision on what to buy.

Take another example: an observer notices a person whistling a tune. Soon they notice how the person next to the whistler starts whistling the same tune. The observer notices this, but the person whistling is unaware that they are copying the other person's tune.

In experience we can clearly see this "perception without awareness" effect through the use of cues or clues. Consider, for instance, the subconscious impact on clients and consumers of pens without chains in banks, fixed coat hangers in hotel rooms, lighting in restaurants, tone of voice in call centers, music in grocery stores. All these provide for fleeting emotional moments which are only felt subconsciously, but are directly impactful on behavior and attitude.

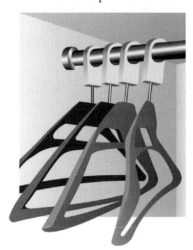

Figure 3.4
What fixed coat hangers tell us

Paco Underhill, in his international bestseller *Why We Buy*, gives numerous practical examples of how the subconscious influences us. For instance, a store removed its carpeting and saw sales plummet. You can imagine how blankly a consumer would look at you if you asked them what the effect of the carpet was on their purchasing behavior!

If this "perception without awareness" is so important to behavior, how then can we understand this side of the experience? Clearly we need a different way of measuring client and consumer response.

One way to do it is this. Rather than ask people to consciously score a survey, we look for how quickly they associate your experience with a word or concept. Based on the speed and accuracy of association, we can define underlying attitudes to (say) a brand. For instance, most people might associate "bad emotion" words such as "dissatisfaction" more readily with a picture of a bank than with a picture of a hospital. It is this difference in association reaction time that picks up the implicit, perceptually held attitude.

In the book *Blink*, Malcolm Gladwell emphasizes the importance of this effect, an effect that uses a research approach called Implicit Association Test (IAT):

IAT is the kind of tool that hits you over the head with its conclusions .... The IAT is more than just an abstract measure of attitudes. It's also a powerful

predictor of how we act in certain kinds of spontaneous situations.
Malcolm Gladwell, *Blink: The power of thinking without thinking*

Yet most market research fails to measure this; traditional explicit techniques pick up conscious reflections but not the subconscious.

For us at Beyond Philosophy, this has been a key omission. The challenge is, though, how do you measure the impact of subconsciously felt experience cues?

This is the focus of the following thought-leading research. It's research that fits well with the chapters later in this book on neuroscience and Customer Experience.

Thought-leadership research: Putting a value on the subconscious

Setting up a website with the help of Dr Peter Jones (of Shire Psychologists) and Dr Nigel Marlow (from London Metropolitan University), with the help of our leading consultants Zhecho Dobrev and Kalina Janevska we aimed to assess the subconscious effect of emotion on a leading cellphone brand (we'll call it Blue Chip here).

Crucially to get to the subconscious, we did not ask customers directly how they felt about Blue Chip on a scale of XYZ. Instead we asked them to categorize a set of emotion words and logos flashed up on a screen into those that they would associate with Blue Chip and those that they would not. If they associated a positive emotion like "happy" more quickly with the Blue Chip than with a competing set of brands, that started to tell us something about the subconscious effect the rival companies had on them. (Note: the actual process was a little more complicated than this simple explanation suggests, but the core idea was to measure the speed of response.)

In addition, we also captured customer attitude scores on standard scales of satisfaction, recommendation and so forth, as well as behavioral scores: that is, ratings based on the time individual customers had spent with Blue Chip on contract and the amount spent per month. This enabled us to model the effect of the subconscious on consumer attitude and behavior.

Results

What we found was that Blue Chip customers' responses to questions on attitude scales such as customer satisfaction – an explicit and conscious reflection on an experience – were not associated with their subconscious emotional experience.

In effect, we found that even though consumers may say they are satisfied with a company, they might subconsciously feel pretty ambivalent towards it.

This is a classic result from IAT, designed to capture not what people say, but what they don't say. It almost acts as a lie detector test! Taking this further, we can surmise that the reason why the academic researcher Sasser found that satisfied customers defect is because they are "not truly satisfied," they just say that they are.

By contrast, when we looked at behavior (tenure and spend), the relationship was clearer. The more a customer spent and the longer their tenure, the faster their speed was on the positive emotional words; and the reverse was true for the negative emotions. In fact we could say:

- A 200 millisecond (mls) speedier response on "happy" was equivalent to 363 days extra tenure and an extra £13 ($20) spend per month with Blue Chip.
- A 200 mls speedier response on "cared for" and "in control" was matched with 584 days extra tenure and an extra £6 ($9) spend per month with Blue Chip.

So when consumers had "skin in the game" – when we looked at their behavior, not just their attitude – they exhibited positive affirming subconsciously held feelings towards the Blue Chip.

Indeed, the extent to which the subconscious explained behavior was much higher than we normally see by explicit conscious survey alone: explaining up to 44 percent of responses in terms of spend per month and 56 percent in terms of tenure. In addition, when we looked at responses from non-Blue Chip consumers, we found, to paraphrase the typical answer: "If, say, I buy O2 (a UK cellphone provider) or Sprint (a US cellphone provider) [both non-buyer examples in this research], then the more satisfied I am with my own supplier, the more negative I feel at the subconscious level towards Blue Chip." In other words, there is a strong subconscious psychological barrier to churn.

Here we are identifying a subconsciously held tribal loyalty. Consumers would never say they have this barrier to switching to an alternative supplier, but in reality they do!

How can it be that there is such a strong relationship between subconscious emotional reaction and consumer behavior? We believe this is because most of our decisions as clients and consumers are driven by "gut reaction"; even seemingly rational decisions are impacted on by the intuitive.

From this research we can now see just how powerful the subconscious emotions can be. It is almost as if we have uncovered the magic dust of research: we need to look at links to behavior, not just attitude. This is something we are all interested in finding, but until now we have been looking in the wrong place.

The subconscious communication model

Putting this research together, we can now start to build a model of how subconscious emotions are communicated. This is shown in Figure 3.5.

Here what we find is that the types of subconsciously felt emotion words used are all concerned with the idea of a power relationship. In other words they reflect control, dominance; not just pleasure or displeasure. We believe this makes intuitive sense when you think about how we look to a brand to guide and direct us to find a better solution. Interestingly these words are not found by asking rational survey questions, demonstrating that the subconscious has a different dynamic.

From this research it became clear that the key subconsciously felt emotions driving value for the Blue Chip mobile company are:

- cared for, pleased, and in control – which drive tenure (and spend per month)
- happy and pleased – which drive spend per month only
- unhappy, annoyed, sluggish, and submissive – which relate to

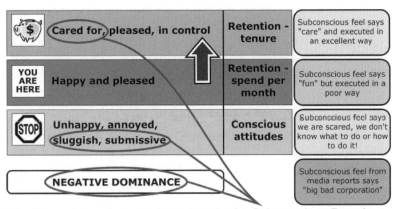

The "Power" emotions are important in the Subconscious Experience

Figure 3.5 The subconscious communication model

consumer attitude (although these words were significant, the effect overall was neutral, so they do not quite destroy the company's value!).

Here the brand needs to focus on emotions such as pleased, cared for, and in control, and how these are communicated at a subconscious level, as these drive the most value, even when the brand's customers are in a "happy, pleased" state. The brand also needs to control how negative emotions (unhappy, annoyed, sluggish, and submissive) are generated and have a subconscious impact on customer behavior. This is in case they become a destructive force. Our research suggested that these were neutral in effect, but they could easily turn negative and destroy the value derived from satisfaction, recommendation, and other attitudinal scores. Finally, we hypothesize the existence of a destructive "negative dominance" state. Fortunately this did not apply to our client, but it occurs when consumers subconsciously think in terms of a "Big Bad Corporation."

What we find in this model is that the types of subconsciously felt emotion words that link to value are analogous to (though not the same as) the Parent–Child relationship in Transactional Analysis (TA). Kalina Janevska, our TA expert, explains:

> Transactional analysis tells us that communication is performed from three positions (ego-states): Adult, Child and Parent. Each of these states is manifested in the way brands and customers communicate; each state being as important as another, although there will be a degree of preference by touch point.
>
> The Blue Chip approaches customers from the Child state: for example, encouraging employees to be friendly, humorous, and relaxed when talking to customers. A more valuable state to evoke is the Parent, where the brand gives customers the sense that they are being taken care of, supported or directed through feedback.

Preparing to climb: get a good Sherpa

You might say to us now, so you have an excellent compass and you understand the geophys. You can lay a path out for me and tell me about lots of different routes, designing the best, quickest, and or most scenic experience. But can you tell me why any particular route is a good one? Can you almost give me a guided tour! Tell me the history of past successes and failures; advise me about the conditions along the journey and critically how to adapt to them. I don't just want to be told that "This is the way."

Even with sophisticated tools you still need your Sherpas to interpret, to find meaning in a subconscious emotion. So we as your Sherpas need, in short, to show you our resumé.

This brings us to our next set of techniques.

Expert interviews – the mind journey resumé

For us, this analogy leads away from the world of stats and more into qualitative research. Yet here too we can take our learnings from psychology, to give depth and meaning to the route. And it is here that we also need experience!

This is why a lot of our clients have found it useful to have an expert interpreter alongside good solid qualitative tools that get behind the meaning of what we quantify. To give you an example, "tone of voice of call center rep" might be the most crucial element that drives emotional and subconscious value in your Customer Experience – but what should you do about it? What does tone of voice mean? Do operatives need a high tone of voice, a low tone of voice, a tone of voice that evokes an emotional reaction only at certain times? What *is* this thing called "tone of voice?"

By using a guide with a good resumé, who can conduct expert interviews either face to face or through group moderation, we can start to understand the emotional and subconscious experience of "tone of voice" as well as many other items.

To give you an example of what this means in terms of technical understanding, we use repertory grid in our interviews.

Repertory grid

This is a specialized interviewing technique, used to uncover the hidden meaning behind experience; getting behind how clients and consumers think and what is truly important to them in their buying decisions. We have seen how consumers and clients tend to answer the "Why did you buy?" question with quite a physical, concrete response. "I bought this sofa because I liked the color." Yet the question you really want to know is a further level up: "The color is important to me because … ."

With rep grid, we are really getting into this hidden subconscious and emotional world. We don't provide a survey form; instead the method lets the interviewees respond to the experience in their own words. The role of the interviewer is to extract the various principles that lie behind these words. For instance, when we tried to understand the snacking experience for a brand of sweet, the degree of "handbagginess" came out as important. In other words, people responded to how clean and easy the sweets were to store in their bag and eat.

If you do not know what your company's Customer Experience is, then this technique is a good starting point. It defines the experience from both the rational and the subconscious/emotional side. This is also an interesting technique by which you can understand how wide of the mark your company is in understanding the experiences of its clients or consumers.

Example business implication: humanics, mechanics, informatics, culturics and formatics

One concept we often use in our work breaks down the elements of an experience into those elements that are derived from human contact (*humanics*) – such as talking to a call center rep – and those that are derived from contact with a process (*mechanics*) – such as the receipt of a utility bill. In addition, we would add three more concepts.

Informatics reflects how an experience is derived from how information is portrayed in (say) written communication such as an email – something that is more than a process but less than a human interface.

Culturics concerns how an experience is derived from a consideration of a client or consumers culture.

Formatics concerns how an experience is derived from how something is aesthetically portrayed. In other words it is a reflection of its form, how the experience is experienced. This is just as important as the function, particularly as we have seen in an earlier chapter when we used the concept of one-second moments.

Visual projectives in our interviews

Sometimes we also use pictures in interviews, asking respondents to select an image from a set that best reflects how they feel. This technique, which falls under the title of "projectives," is useful because in many instances people find it easier to describe how they feel in pictures than through discussion. Similar techniques include projective questioning, which takes the general form of "If company X were an animal, what

46

animal would it be?" and is used with psychological techniques to help understand how analogies and metaphors are used.

In our work we have used visual impressions to help interviewees describe their feelings towards an experience. For instance, when we map the customer journey we ask interviewees to discuss their journey through pictures. The advantage of this is that it pulls out subconscious feelings which might not be accessible, or would be muted, in verbal description, as well as uncovering how consumers feel about sensitive issues they might be unwilling to talk about directly.

Visual impressions effectively open the mind to a different way of expressing an experience. As an example of this, in working with a construction company we found that images of slickness – in a negative way – came through from our nonverbal techniques. This had not been apparent in the face-to-face verbal interviews.

When you think about it, we understand things not just verbally but through visual imagery. These techniques get to access that understanding, providing a unique and different insight.

Text mining in our qualitative analysis

Another technique we use focuses on the conscious and subconscious messages consumers pick up about a company through the media – whether through the written word, or from the look and feel of coverage.

One way we use to assess these messages is simply by photographing resonant experiences. We look at the material and try to identify some of the ways in which firms manipulate their image, which might subconsciously affect those who see the material. In addition, we also look at the messages delivered by the written word. Here we use sophisticated text mining tools (using neural networks) to identify the most resonant key words, on which we can focus our qualitative analysis of "affects." An example of this is the way in which we looked at how promoters and detractors talk to each other over time.

> By surveying open-ended commentaries over time, we can see how change occurs and how the market evolves. So during the sales season all the talk could be about price, while at another point the voice of the crowd could be talking about a new design coming out. This enables you to capture trends before they go mainstream! In this way we are picking up and owning trends that are still not out yet.

One new way to do this is to *crowd source*, dipping into the words people use at various points in time, and then asking the crowd to vote on what is the most representative comment.

Blogs and Twitter are interesting new sources to assess how your clients and customers are talking about your company. We will discuss this further in the chapters on social media.

Preparing to climb: communication tools

So far we have spoken a lot about guiding you up the mountain – but what if you get lost? What if, as the wind blows and the snow reforms the landscape, what you see is not quite what the map says? Clearly a walkie-talkie would be good here. Then you could make decisions on the spot. In much the same way, a market is a dynamic force. Things change all the time, new products and services emerge, and unforeseen events change our perceptions.

In our context, then, we need a walkie-talkie to help us understand in depth both how consumers might react to a change – understand their goal map – and how events occur "in the moment." If we enable excellent and near-real time communication ,and understand how our mountaineers might react, we can quickly adapt to changed conditions.

In-the-moment research: The mind journey walkie-talkie

Goal mapping

Consumers at each and every stage of their journey are motivated by the goals they seek. These form a hierarchy, from the tactical action-oriented goals of day-to-day living through to the strategic desires that sit behind much of what we do. If we can understand these goals we have a route into differentiating our offer, based on the highest levels of motivation. For instance, why did so many people choose IBM in the early days of computing? On the face of it, it might have seemed that purchasing from IBM was about product and pricing features. In reality, though, many other companies offered computers with better pricing or features. People chose IBM because what was of most concern to them was the feeling that they were reducing risk in a field that was scary and unfamiliar by picking the market leader. They didn't want to fail in their jobs through incorrect supplier selection, and "no one ever got fired for buying IBM."

If we are aware of goals like these, then we can create the right experience, even if there is a fundamental shift in the corporate envi-ronment. Likewise, if we hold such a "goal map" of what customers want, we also have in effect an audit tool for things such as business process re-engineering (BPR). For instance, Figure 3.6 is a goal map

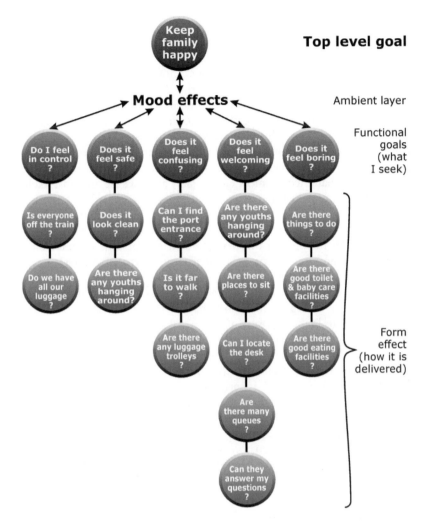

Figure 3.6 Goal mapping at a ferry port

for a ferry journey, based, from experience diaries, on one moment of contact – a family entering a port facility.

Of course, this is a very simplified goal map, but we can still draw some useful lessons from it.

First, consumer goals are often built around asking "risk management questions." In other words people are thinking, perhaps subconsciously, is something bad going to happen? This goal to mitigate risk is like our flight or fight reflex. This also means we tend to look for things not in our experience. We are conditioned to think, "Are there drunken youths hanging around the port?" and to worry about other hazards. The ability to notice the negative moment is hard-wired into the brain.

The second effect is to do with the "how." For instance, how is the entrance signposted? How does the entrance look? The visual expression is just as important as the functional goals.

As we move up the hierarchy we come to the "functional goals layer," which concerns how our overall impressions are interpreted from our goals into emotions. These emotions are important for action and learning. In our brains, emotions help to imprint key information, so the things that affect us most emotionally are ones we are most likely to remember the next time.

Fourth comes mood effects. These are interesting as they are not so pointedly "goal directed." They create an ambience that affects how strongly we feel. This can be strong, and it can be either negative or positive. So the wow factor of a super-clean port can moderate our negative emotions if the ship leaves late.

Finally, there is the top-level goal to which everything is directed; in this case, it is keeping the family happy, which is, let's face it, the ultimate goal in life for most of us.

A goal map like this can also help in product and service design – not just in an audit capacity, but highlighting possible new creative ways we could change the experience. If the ultimate goal is "keep the family happy," then entertainment is certainly a ploy to be considered, even if it is not in the experience today.

And as we have seen with BPR and Six Sigma (where the changes are aligned to a cost-cutting agenda), such a formalized mapping process can also better embed the customer view within an established process, acting as an audit function. After all to quote Hamel and Prahalad in *Competing for the Future*, "You can't shrink to greatness."

In-the-moment research

Capturing momentary effects as they occur across the journey is perhaps the great gap in research today: although this is fortunately not true for experience psychology research. For instance, at Beyond Philosophy we use experience diaries and photography (where applicable), aiming to capture a "stream of consciousness" from customers and clients, not their reflections. Here is an example. You will notice that these experience diaries capture not so much the verbal as the verbal *and* the visual from customers at the point of decision making:

> When deciding on insurance, the difference between providers is often very slight. I certainly choose a provider I know just because it feels less risky,

but at the end of the day I base my decision within those few competitors I know and have a good product, on the warmth I get at the end of the phone. Does it sound like a person I can trust? Is there a good look and feel to the brochure? Do they understand me? Sometimes this can be a delayed decision: for instance I'm tied to a provider but I'll go with you next year.

Competitive differentiators: Soft sounding rep voice, understanding of my situation, forgiving of my previous crash, warmth/expensive look of brochure, and speed of response (perhaps too speedy though).

Capturing and understanding these "moments of affect" is by no means an easy task, but the effort is worthwhile. The experience diary cuts to the chase, revealing some of the impressions wrought by the "experience of you," and also how to avoid undermining your corporate values, for instance through a poorly chosen tone of voice.

Likewise, in the near future the integration of new online technology as consumers and clients become online all the time means that in-the-moment research has the potential to fundamentally alter how research is conducted. Steven has a good example of this:

Today more and more people have smart phones with internet access. Today they are BlackBerrys or iphones, but tomorrow this could be as simple as wearable devices. All this opens the way for a more instant form of survey response.

For instance, customers can use a phone to record their experience and send their reflections to a website. And of course this can work the opposite way: rather than just provide feedback, customers can pick up a voucher from the same website and give their views on new designs. At last the survey is no longer a static thing but interactive, and not just real-time but real-life! To a certain extent this is already happening with text feedback.

Alternatively, perhaps I'm an employee of the restaurant. Now not only can I get real time in-the-moment feedback to respond to, but perhaps I too could give my reflections, texted or otherwise to an online site.

Not only is this research in an instant, this is also now engaging participation. We are no longer talking about survey reports propping up doors, but a means of client–customer and employee engagement. We are also perhaps seeing how events in the moment are not quite as rational or static as we assumed them to be! In this way we can find greater ways to differentiate ourselves from the competition and find out what is really going on in the mind of the consumer.

Instead of corporate reports coming down from head office, there is now, and will be even more in the future, a genuine opportunity to create localism and actionability in research. It's a virtuous circle of real-life data from customers and employees married to immediate feedback.

Preparing to climb: a team with ideas!

Our final experience psychology research technique relates to the "what if" scenario. What if as we climbed our mountain a sudden snowstorm blew or an avalanche occurred? How would we manage? This then relates to our creative skill, how we can design "on the fly." This is actually far more important than most businesses realize. When you think about it, everything starts with "the idea," yet there is so much emphasis on analysis and measurement that most businesses completely underestimate the importance of managing their creative equity.

Manage your creative equity – the support crew

Beyond Philosophy enables this side of the corporate brain through research, which means creative workshops, incentivized ideas schemes, even imagineering departments to ensure empowerment of the process. Critically this means providing an approach that enables what we call your "Magicians." These are those people in an organization, as likely at the bottom of the corporate hierarchy as at the top, who are natural experts at generating strategic and tactical ideas. For example consider the strange case of Maurice Ward. In the early 1990s he invented a material called Starlite. In tests conducted by NASA this was shown to be able to withstand temperatures as high as those found in a nuclear flash without any signs of melting. On the BBC science program *Tomorrow's World* an egg was coated with the substance and withstood the temperature of an acetylene torch. Scientific studies proved that it worked, and many firms eagerly awaited the release of Starlite. Yet Maurice Ward had no professional scientific background and had for the previous two decades earned a living as a ladies' hairdresser.

Unfortunately the story does not have a happy ending. So far, no product based on Starlite has been released to the market. Apart from the obvious question – whatever happened to Starlite? (a mystery you might want to try to find out for us!) – another important issue is, where did the idea come from? A company investigation revealed the following:

> One of the outcomes of this was an investigation by ICI's paints laboratory that the most significantly qualified of its research chemists had contrib-

uted to the least number of patents. The fewer the scientific qualifications staff possessed, the greater the number of patents they had contributed to. The person who had contributed to most ICI's patents had no scientific qualifications at all.

In managing your creative equity, then, you need to use research techniques that communicate with the whole organization, something that we effectively do with our Moment Mapping® tools. Here we conduct ideas workshops open to everyone in the company. But we should also be cognisant of the fact that Magicians often work alone, which is why it is important to support ideas "as they happen" in the organization through effectively run ideas schemes alongside more ad-hoc creative workshops.

Manage your creative equity as much as your analytical resources. It is, after all, often those closest to the ground who can create the most value for you and come up with the best ideas, ideas that offer the opportunity to not just follow but potentially lead the group psychology. Unfortunately in most walks of life it is analytical equity that predominates. Yet the skills sets are related and different. To excel in analysis does not necessarily mean to excel creatively, and vice versa. Think about how the Beatles music was written by performers who could not read music, or how Einstein had to get a job as a patent clerk because he could not get a prestigious university posting. The history of ideas is replete with examples of creative genius not quite matched by technical, analytical capability. And so it is with the firm: it is not the analytical equity alone that will help differentiate your firm.

Your Sherpa

Experience psychology research is about understanding the emotional and the subconscious world of the client or consumer, and how they might perceive the experience your organization offers. This in turn requires turning your customer insight research processes into experience psychology research: a process that requires specialist techniques, expert guidance, and a different philosophy. For as much as we want an intuitive understanding of our customers and clients, we want to enable firms through research also to be able to act creatively and intuitively. In summary, Table 3.1 gives some of the key questions you can answer by turning to experience psychology research.

Experience psychology research techniques bring approaches to the market that bring us closer to defining the value of Customer Experience, something that has always been a problem because current techniques are so rationally based.

In our final future trend we now turn our attention to how firms can impact "group psychology." This means looking at creating a group-sense around your marketing, using the psychology of the group or community to which you belong, to encourage greater emotional engagement with your clients and consumers.

Table 3.1 Some key questions and how experience psychology can help answer them

Key question	Experience psychology techniques
■ What is our organization's customer experience?	■ Use expert interviews: think about using a repertory grid to uncover the hidden and visible components of an experience.
■ How much value (conscious, emotional, subconscious) can we get from changing our customer experience?	■ Use Emotional Signature®. ■ Consider emotional segmentation.
■ How should we change our experience?	■ Use Emotional Signature®. ■ Look at design for emotion techniques.
■ How important are the subconscious impressions consumers hold of us?	■ Use the subconscious communication model.
■ What are the goals our consumers seek?	■ Undertake goal mapping.
■ What is the gap between what we believe the experience is and what our customers believe it to be?	■ Use a repertory grid between the provider of a product or service and a replicated study against customers.
■ What information do customers and clients pick up and use about us?	■ Use text mining techniques, following your market through time and ethnographic in-the-moment research.

4 Community marketing

The new marketing will be about community: small or large groups of people who come together in some shared interest. This means that consideration will increasingly have to be given to how we target these groups, not just the individual.

Consider how for instance Cerritos Library was designed as a shopping mall to impart a familiar sense of community to the hard-to-reach 12–25 age groups. Likewise, think of how a winery in Surrey, England extended beyond the sale of wine to the provision of services in tune with its core audience, the affluent over-60s. Now the winery offers fine dining and evening light classical concerts, essentially finding a group reference point by which to differentiate an offering. Now "I feel" they are part of my community!

Professor Hugh Wilson from Cranfield School of Management further highlights how this sense of community was designed into the London Symphony Orchestra (LSO), in order to differentiate it from other orchestras:

> We found that LSO concert-goers went for "soul-food," finding the music a spiritual, uplifting experience. In this, the high standards of the orchestra were serving it well. For most, though, concert-going was also a social experience: a good night out with friends.
>
> Importantly, these relational needs were found to extend to concert-goers' relationship with performers. Regular supporters in particular felt part of the orchestra, taking a pride in the orchestra's work in the same way that football supporters discuss how well "we" played in the last game.
>
> These insights led to some immediate ideas for fine-tuning the concert experience. The post-concert experience could be improved by keeping a well-advertised area of the center buzzing in the hour after the concert. Community could be facilitated by members of the orchestra coming on rota to the nominated bar after the concert to chat to concert-goers.

Perhaps it is because of the rise of social media, which we cover in the next chapters, but it feels as if marketing and research is now going beyond understanding the individual, towards understanding inter-relationships between individuals, how people connect together, how

55

we react as a group, and what that means in terms of services and products.

In this chapter, then, we look at the group and how we can manage it from an experience psychology perspective. This means keeping in front of the "herd instinct" and the psychology of the pack, as well as avoiding its pitfalls: the classic example of this is the credit crunch. To quote the former chairman of Ulster Bank, Sir George Quigley (from the *Irish Times*), "banks were driven by 'herd instinct' into reckless lending due to the highly competitive banking environment in which they operated over recent years."

First we look at fashion, whether an organization looks in or out of fashion to the group. Then we will consider how it can lead the group, creating a sense of relationship to the group that goes beyond the brand sense of individuals. Finally, we look at perhaps the most critical aspect, the internal group: how businesses not only need to reflect the concerns of their audience through the clues and heuristics they impart, but also how the Employee Experience is maintained.

Are you fashionable?

Sometimes running a business can make you feel like an ant walking up a sandhill. You know where you want to go, but small movements in the ground beneath your feet undermine your every step. It's like those almost imperceptible changes in social mood or group psychology that trip us up unexpectedly, the classic example of this being economic changes in business confidence. This is something that may not have happened at an individual level, but is most certainly felt as a group trend.

What we are focused on, then, is how firms can keep a foothold in a constantly evolving world. If previous chapters have been about using experience psychology to help us understand and respond to the emotional and subconscious needs of the client or consumer as an individual, this chapter is about how we respond in experience psychology terms to group effects.

To illustrate the point, this is about whether you are picking up on the broad psychological concerns of the group. Are you tuned in to their Zeitgeist (the spirit of the times)?

Consider for instance how "green" and "ethical" concerns have been used by the Fair Trade movement, how Ben & Jerry's was positioned towards social activism, and with the credit crunch, how the more successful firms have shown a psychological understanding, repositioning themselves on price. In the United Kingdom for instance, large grocery retailers Asda and Sainsbury's are renowned for their responsiveness to change. They introduced a 14p toothpaste with the recession, while Morrisons, another UK retailer, brought in "Let's grow" vouchers encourage children to do gardening, picking up on the green trend.

Ethics, being green, recession marketing: these might not be of concern to us as individuals, but they speak to us as members of society. And they work because they act at that emotional and subconscious level. Demonstrating that you care is in group terms a powerful motivator.

But that is not the end of the story. It is not just about big economic shifts or the latest global concern; it is also and perhaps more importantly about the aesthetic. If you don't follow your industry "fashion" you can suddenly find yourself at odds with the world. Steven Walden gives us an example:

> This is sometimes about imperceptible changes in customers' group psychology that change the "flavor" of what you are dealing with, and consequently how you are perceived. The risk is, of course, that if you do not keep pace, you can suddenly find yourself floundering. After all we all either subconsciously or consciously want to fit in; none of us want to be left on the outside! Wearing flared trousers and high-soled shoes might have looked "in" during the mid-1970s but it's decidedly "out" today!

Figure 4.1 How fashionable are you?

> So ask yourself the question, how fashionable are you? Are you keeping up with what is in and what is out, with the Zeitgeist, or spirit of the times?

Consider for instance how this notion of following fashion is a key driver to store revamps, as has recently occurred with McDonald's, or in a less successful way the plethora of brand relaunches with names ending in .com at the end of the 1990s. Or how about the way an experience is communicated through the written word? We all know subconsciously how typographic styles change, so 1980s fonts and design look 1980s, and 1960s fonts and design look 1960s.

In a business-to-business context this kind of effect is just as resonant, demonstrating that group psychology is not just transmitted in the consumer-related industries. One of the best ways to see this is to look back at marketing history and consider how things have evolved. For instance, an ex-marketing director of a leading UK construction company told us this about his experiences during the 1980s:

> In construction we introduced mobile phones and computers into the workplace .... When we first heard about this, it was mooted as a way to save money and raise productivity, but it was nothing more than a belief, there was no evidence. But you see what happens is, things gradually evolve. People start talking about it, then someone is first to jump in, and everyone feels they must follow otherwise they'll lose ground. Certainly none of us knew what would actually happen. It's all trial and error, it all happens gradually at first, and then in a short space of time once the psychological belief is there, we all have these IT systems in place. Of course, we were the first to have this, and lost a lot of money, as XXX [a large computer company] didn't know what they were doing. But that's learning for you, the next client got a better system, as XXX could go around after and say, we now know how to do this!
>
> Unsurprisingly, the cost savings promised never happened, but once we all had this way of working in place, the whole environment and way of doing things had altered. Now I had a mobile phone and could be caught any time during the day! The older guys didn't like it but the younger ones soon latched on that this was the way of doing things.

In this example we can see how a belief and a technology-led business case become a fashion, which in turn leads to an entirely new working environment, often accepted and taken up by the younger generation; and as they start to progress up the corporate ladder, so they take this new psychology with them. Critically this effect, the follow-my-leader imperative driving the new fashion, means that no one can afford to be left behind. In effect, what starts as an offensive means of gaining competitive advantage becomes a defensive strategy to remain with the pack, until it becomes a norm.

Yes, it is easy to see how an accountancy argument could have been put forward to stop investing in the new and unproven, yet if it feels like the way of the future, feels as if others could go down that route and threaten your position – well then, it must be done! Quite frankly, another key driver is that people just get tired of the same old, same old.

In all those business cases based on financial return, perhaps the most important issue is not whether the organization will gain X amount if it invests in something, but rather whether it might lose Y if it doesn't; a significant case for understanding where the herd is going. After all, no one wants to talk to a fashion victim wearing the trends of a decade ago. Nothing is more obvious, nothing is more unappealing, however good you are at doing business.

Leading the herd

Be the first to occupy the mind space of a new trend!

Unfortunately, too often companies end up as me-too followers of a group effect. A competitor offers a green solution, so they feel they need to roll out their own. Yet a bigger advantage can be had if companies aim at leading the group psychology. Consider for instance the Toyota Prius, the Red Card (American Express) or at a more aesthetic level, the look and feel of a Virgin brochure or bill.

Ideally what you are aiming for is to develop a corporate psyche to which customers feel some degree of attachment at a group emotional or subconscious level. For instance, there are certain companies that go beyond their brand: they have "sense of community," bringing us together as a group of consumers who share a common bond.

Coke is more than a fizzy drink; IBM is more than an IT system vendor; Tesco and Walmart (large grocery chains in respectively the United Kingdom and United States) are more than grocery stores; Apple is more than a computer retailer. The list goes on, their relationship to the group being less about the brand and the features of the product or service sold (profoundly individual customer effects) and more about the connection people feel as a group.

By way of example, this effect was demonstrated when in the 1980s Coke tried to change its taste. Even though only 10–12 percent of focus group interviewees said that they would not drink Coke in the new formula, they were vociferous enough in their protest to put peer pressure on the broader social group, and soon it started to "feel" as if customers should be against the new Coke. Mostly this was not about the taste, but about the historical association customers had with the brand. In other words, Coke in its original formulation had psychological resonance with the group, an emotional and subconscious connection that, as was later to be shown, offered an excellent platform for product diversification.

Organizations with such a community sense then lever their subconscious and emotional relationship with their customer groups as a route to growth. In essence, they are aware of how their customer groups want

Table 4.1 Companies that build on community psychology

Company	Community psychological feel
Tesco and Walmart	■ Trusted, family-friendly
IBM	■ Trusted, secure
Starbucks	■ Ethical, eco-friendly
Harley-Davidson	■ Tough, idiosyncratic
Apple	■ Hip, innovative

to feel when they do business with them. If you like, they are closely in touch with the key archetypal images that represent the group aspiration: for instance the tough, idiosyncratic biker (Harley-Davidson) or the ethical, cosmopolitan, eco-friendly consumer (Starbucks).

Table 4.1 gives some examples of how companies have developed a community feel. From this we can see that Tesco, Walmart, IBM, Apple, Starbucks, Virgin, and Harley-Davidson all grow and expand through the way they express emotional and subconsciously felt associations with their customer groups. Speak about Apple, for instance, and the group identifies with a sense of the hip and innovative. The advantage comes in that this is a far more powerful platform for growth than say Another Computer Retailer that expresses me-too service capabilities alone.

Likewise, Tesco's expansion into non-grocery lines such as financial services is consequent on this "bigger than the service" psychological relationship. If target customers as a group perceive a company as trustworthy and family-friendly, that closeness is abstract enough that it can extend its business line – although clearly within the confines of its category (in this case retailing).

Building a community organization not only keeps customer groups loyal, it also differentiates your company from those still competing on their product or service alone!

From an experience psychology point of view, to manage group psychology it is important therefore to uncover the sense clients and consumers get of your company. Critically the starting point for such work should be the identification of those segments that are important to the company, as it is the opinions of these groups that will formulate its future experience, as we saw in the cases of Cerritos Library and Harley-Davidson. It is by leading from these groups that you pull "the herd" with you. Act the leader and others will follow.

Then you need to conduct a "psychological audit," a survey approach that reflects how it "feels" amongst this group to interact with your organization. Typically this involves use of our experience psychology research techniques. For instance, we can determine the subconsciously felt emotion words customers attach to their experience of the organization, and come to understand through our social communication model what kind of relationship exists at the emotional and subconscious level.

Creating the fashionable organization

Once you have understood the sense that needs to be portrayed, the next step is to spread the right psychological cues within your organization. This means displaying the correct messages. Consider for instance the "7 percent–38 percent–55 percent rule" of Albert Mehrabian, and how this might relate to how your firm feels to a client or consumer group:

According to Mehrabian, three elements account differently for our liking for the person who puts forward a message concerning their feelings. Words account for 7 percent, tone of voice accounts for 38 percent, and body language accounts for 55 percent of the liking. These are often abbreviated as the "Three Vs": Verbal, Vocal and Visual.[1]

Using this as an analogy, 55 percent is about the visual appeal of an organization, 38 percent is about how it sounds – think of call center operatives' tone of voice – and just 7 percent involves the words it uses. This means that any psychologically relevant message needs to focus less on the written content of communication than on the way it is put across.

This consideration of the aesthetic, the look and feel fashion elements of an experience, includes for instance the classic example of corporate branding. Consider how De Walt uses black and yellow color schemes in its branding; traditionally these are the "accepted" colors of the construction trade.

If this puts the emphasis on look and feel, we should also not forget the power of story-telling: how psychological messages can be spread through an organization by example. For instance, US credit card companies Capital One and American Express are great at doing this, embedding personal customer stories in internal literature and across the working environment. These might look a little hackneyed, but the point is that this is the start of a process.

Likewise, understanding how close the corporate group psychology is to the sense you want customers to get of the organization is an important and much under-considered area. It is no good talking about consumers feeling the organization is "hip and innovative" if the internal group psyche is professional and boring.

---

1   Source: Wikipedia references for Professor Mehrabian.

The Employee Experience

This brings us to our next key point, that managing group psychology is as much about managing the internal dynamics of your organization, the interpersonal relationship side, the ability to create new ideas, as it is about analyzing and understanding customer feedback.

Indeed, one of the things that differentiates experience psychology from consumer psychology is its emphasis on the Employee Experience. Why? Because the organization's Customer Experience is directly reflected in the attitudes and behavior of its staff: how they are treated, empowered, and feel about working for the organization.

At the end of the day the emphasis should be on empowerment. After all, not only is it true to say that "Those who don't make decisions don't make mistakes," it is also true that risk taking is the key way in which firms develop, learn, and innovate. Take this out and firms will end up narrowly defined and more at risk of losing market share. Avoiding risk also creates a very poor working environment, with a reduced emphasis on where the value-in-use of an organization really lies!

Understanding the Employee Experience is as important to an organization as how it markets its products or services.

So what to do?

For us, the key to creating a better Employee Experience is to break down any disconnect between teams. This means understanding and getting to grips with the qualitative "shadow side" of employment: in other words, interpersonal relations. Unfortunately, too often this proves too much for leadership, and managers who focus more on a destructive accountancy mentality of poor balanced scorecards and bad measurements which have the effect of driving negative behavior and undermining social capital. A classic example is some uses of the internal market. On paper and in theory it sounds great: each business unit only does work for other units that is paid for and profitable. In reality if used unwisely it can undermine the relationship side of a business.

Beware therefore of turning management into target management, the type of disruptive activity that means that rather than leading from the front and being directly engaged in a learning culture, companies become atomized and a sense of responsibility is lost. The message becomes, it's your target; I'm not interested. That is not to say that targets don't count. They can be highly motivating, but you need to connect them with building relationships, not creating barriers between people – which means they must be flexible, realistic, and part of a learning culture.

Be clear, then: for us it is the development of this interpersonal relationship side that drives business success: nothing more, nothing less.

Using experience psychology research

In our work we have been fortunate to do a number of studies on employee engagement. From this we have found an unfortunate tendency for Human Resources to follow the traditional research approach: measure the rational. It sometimes seems as if no one is measuring how employees feel about the organization!

So as a first step, we would encourage you to find out your employees' Emotional Signature® and subconsciously felt perceptions. This means understanding their positive and negative emotions, what drives these feelings, what you can do about it, and whether there are any key segments of the workforce who like or dislike the organization. For instance, you might find that the brand or customer experience values that the organization is trying to evoke are actually not subconsciously perceived by staff; alternatively, you might find that your most valuable staff are the least emotionally engaged.

We also suggest that in order to see how group effects change with time and how the internal culture needs to adapt, there should be an emphasis on real-time measurement, understanding "how we are doing" and where the big wins and failings are in the organization's approach across the key touch points. An example is how British Airways have embedded this in their processes:

> One way of prioritizing is simply to look at what specific event satisfactions correlate highly with outcomes such as overall satisfaction and positive word-of-mouth. In the difficult aviation market since 2001, British Airways has used this approach to fine-tune which aspects of the customer journey are most important to the customer.
>
> Professor Hugh Wilson, Cranfield School of Management

We also see that internally research needs to become more action oriented. It is no good research sitting as a siloed function and being ignored, it needs to be in the corporate bloodstream. So as we move to embed experience psychology in an organization – we would say that customer insights must now embrace the new emotional and subconscious research techniques and that we need to ensure actionability on the ground.

This orientation has some of the feel of the participatory action research currently used in parts of the developing world, where the research process is embedded at ground level for groups to learn from experience amongst themselves. In essence, feedback from customers becomes part of the learning individual groups use to improve their performance.

Likewise, we are firm believers in the "get out there and see what it's like" approach. Immerse yourself in what it is like to be a client or customer. Using your intuition to understand what is right or wrong about an experience is a valid approach.

Ultimately, you want to build an emotionally engaged community of interest around your employees as much as around your customers. One that is realistically aligned to customer expectations and does not suffer from "groupthink": that is to say a misalignment between what employees think the Customer Experience is, and what customers actually say it is!

The dangers of groupthink

If you understand your Employee Experience you can not only improve it, but also see how customer-centric it is. For instance, how about comparing how your customers see the organization and how employees see it? We did this in our work with a leading transport company. We undertook a comparison, using a psychological technique called rep grid, between in-company attitudes towards the firm, identifying what it was good and bad at in comparison with its competitors, and what customers thought of it. What was interesting about this exercise was the gap between the employee belief that it achieved customer service excellence and the lack of any validation from consumers. There was also a strong level of agreement that the company was transactional – competing on price and speed of service – but limited agreement on the value-in-use angle. Customers noticed how they were handled more than the company did.

The benefit of this approach is to make real and quantitative the gap between company thinking and customer thinking. Know this and you can better align your internal corporate thinking with your customers.

And for employees we do not forget the importance of co-creation, how in product and service design it is important to involve stakeholders as much as guide and direct them to what management wants.

Building community through the channels

Co-creation is an example of building psychological resonance between stakeholders. Here rather than thinking of separate supplier–customer–company groups, companies are trying to create a psychological closeness. Now rather than being separate groups, the aim is to treat all stakeholders as one group, in it together. Both Build-a-Bear and Southwest Airlines in their B2B relationships demonstrate this capability to bring groups together:

A lot of suppliers don't just want to sell more products; they want to work with you to come up with the most creative ideas to sell products. We brainstorm a lot with our vendors, but a lot of what they want is to be a part of the story and the planning. So some of it is just about kindness and respect. To evoke this we work very fairly with our suppliers, we give them notice about what we are doing and what we want to do, which gives them a big opportunity to participate at whatever level they want. If people need their payment earlier than they originally intended because of some business opportunity or issue, then we would go along with that. We also try to make everyone a part of our company and share in our success.

Maxine Clark, CEO Build-a-Bear

Our suppliers were part of the family. We always tried to negotiate with people who understood our "family" values. As an example, we gave them T-shirts and invited them to our corporate events, sent them cards on their birthdays, etc. One time I even negotiated rates with a company that I really wanted to do business with as they had a good product and reliable reputation. I realized that they didn't understand the type of long-term relationships we wanted, and they undercut their pricing so badly that I looked at them and said, "Guys, you are not going to make it for long with pricing like this, and I want you to be here long term, so let's go ahead and renegotiate this and make it more money. Let's make it a win-win." We always try to see a relationship as a win-win; it was never just about "Let's get the best price." That would infer we didn't care about what happens to them. We always intended for our relationships to be long term at Southwest.

Lorraine Grubbs-West, ex-VP, Southwest Airlines (from *Lessons in Loyalty*)

> Becoming one group makes people more emotionally committed.
> It is to this emotional and subconscious effect that we must
> look to create new value and maintain bonds that are difficult
> to break or imitate.

The global community

Trends to 2100

There is a famous clip taken from an old BBC program, *Tomorrow's World*. A boss dictates a letter to "his" secretary before it is sent by computer. Prescient, absolutely – except it doesn't quite ring true, does it? Why? Because technological change goes hand in hand with social change – each one affects the other.

We have already seen how in experience psychology terms we are starting to think about marketing to the group. But beyond that there is a deeper trend. This is the trend towards global community: how problems in one part of the world become everyone's concerns; how issues such as ethics and global warming will affect how we psychologically perceive the actions of any organization.

We live in an increasingly interconnected world, something we will learn more about in the next chapter. The Web is changing everything. The relationship that is global and virtual will also become critical. Consumer trends occurring in China or New Zealand will now have the potential to be as influential on our buying patterns in the virtual world as any local trend. In effect our virtual universe will become our community.

For the firm, in thinking about experience psychology in the future, there needs to be a focus on two divergent themes. One is how to show a human face, how to demonstrate relationships, especially online – if you like, how to make the organization feel local. Yet at the same time it needs to embrace a multifaceted, multicultural, multi-everything world: if you like, it also needs to come across as globally relevant.

Super-nicheing may be one strategy: personalization taken to the extreme, where what customers want now becomes fed into the superhighway, and the end result is the perfectly tailored solution delivered to their door. This is potentially bad news for big firms, as the future economy becomes virtualized and about joining together diverse, almost cottage, industries to get a combined solution. Indeed, the psychology of the experience will now become focused less on brand recognition and more on the personal interface created to help people through the morass of virtual companies "there to help." Perhaps the qualities of a "virtual assistant" will ultimately be what it is really about.

We also see potential for experiential marketing, with the increasing use of sensory clues. For instance, how about sitting in your living room and being able to turn the room into a desert island at the click of a switch? Putting chips in everything is now the new wallpaper.

Therefore, we are beginning to see what will ultimately be a move to a more diverse, do-what-you-want world: one where you will not be put into silos, go to university at this age, work in an office, retire at this age. As age and illness is itself tackled, people will increasingly sense a mood of freedom. Sure, we'll still have to earn a living, but it could be a living made at home, with more human contact coming from virtual and hence global communities.

So let's talk a bit more about the Web and social media, and their role in the future Customer Experience.

5 Social media: the birth of a new channel to market

We are living in historic times. The Web is still in its infancy and yet it is fundamentally changing everything around us. Yet we are still only at the beginning of the digitization of everything! In fact things are moving so fast that one of the challenges of writing a book in old "traditional media" is that these statistics will be out of date by the time you are reading this, but they will still blow your mind:[1]

- Americans have access to 1,000,000,000,000 webpages.
- Unique readers of online newspapers are up by 30,000,000.
- Movie video uploaded to YouTube in the last two months is greater than the combined content from ABC, NBC, and CBS since 1948.
- ABC, NBC, and CBS collectively have 10,000,000 unique visitors each month. MySpace, YouTube and Facebook have 250,000,000 collectively each month. These sites didn't exist six years ago.
- 95 percent of music downloads are not paid for.
- Wikipedia hosts 13,000,000 articles in 200 languages.
- Dell claims to have earned US$6.5 million (£4 million) from Twitter posts since 2007.

Americans nearly tripled the amount of time they spend on social networking and blog sites such as Facebook and MySpace between 2009 and 2010.[2] In August 2009, 17 percent of all time spent on the internet was at social networking sites, up from 6 percent in August 2008. For the first time in 23 years Pepsi decided not to have an ad during the SuperBowl and instead use the funds on internet campaigns, with US$20 million going to social media.[3]

---

1 http://www.youtube.com/watch?v=6ILQrUrEWe8&feature=player_embeddedDid you know video4.0
2 http://blog.nielsen.com/nielsenwire/online_mobile/social-networking-and-blog-sites-capture-more-internet-time-and-advertisinga/
3 http://abcnews.go.com/Business/pepsis-big-gamble-ditching-super-bowl-social-media/story?id=9402514

Looking back to the birth of television in the 1950s you will realize the world was a much more synchronized place than it is today.[4] People used to watch the same television programs at the same time, on very similar models of television set. When we were at school all our friends used to watch *Monty Python's Flying Circus,* and the following day they would recite the sketches. However today, the brave new world of content abundance, where YouTube has more content that traditional television programs, has enable people to free their individuality. This content is also instantly available, anywhere, anytime, prompting a massive decline in traditional media and a massive uptake in the use of content online. Why would you want a newspaper that tells you yesterday's news?

In the heyday before the internet the world was owned by the mass media. If you had enough money you could sell anything; all you needed to do was buy enough advertising space. The technology, whether television, radio, or newspapers, meant the same message was delivered to the masses. This meant the messages were designed for the masses, not for individuals. This "mass" mindset was also driven by the manufacturing world, which at the time was not sophisticated enough to create individual or personalized products. Manufacturing technology was such that everything had to be the same to create economies of scale. "You can have any car that you want as long as it's black," Henry Ford famously told everyone. Ironically, it is this standardization of products and mass messages, its very ubiquity, that is one of the death knells for this type of approach.

This approach drives commoditization, which eventually means a lack of differentiation, and when everything is the same, people turn to price. Cutting prices then affects profitability. Our very own founder, Colin Shaw's first pioneering book on the Customer Experience in 2002, *Building Great Customer Experiences,* extolled the virtues of focusing on the experience as a differentiator.

It is only since the 1980s and 1990s that personalization and customization have come about in manufacturing. Dell is a good example. Dell changed the way PCs were manufactured by offering customized solutions: you could choose how big you wanted your hard disc, what processor should be used, and so on. This led to Dell being voted one of the most admired companies in the United States a few years ago. Any rise is quickly followed by a fall. In the early 2000s Dell has been better known for "Dell sucks." It went through problems in customer service, and more and more people discovered they were not the only customers having problems. The Web helped facilitate that discovery. A quick Google search today (October 2009) revealed 2,710,000 hits for

---

4 http://www.longtailbook.com

"Dell sucks." This shows the scale of the customer service challenges Dell have experienced.

History shows us there have been four big changes in communications:[5]

- the printing press
- the telephone
- the ability to record things
- television.

All of these are "one to many" media. The internet and social media are the next change. These are the first forms of media that are "many to many." This is significant, and is shifting power from companies to consumers. Today anyone can communicate with many people free of charge, meaning the general public have a voice, a medium in which they can communicate that rivals the voice of big companies. They have a medium that they can use to publicize good and bad customer experiences. We are witnessing a historic shift in the way organizations deal with customers, the "democratization of journalism," as some people call it. Too many organizations do not see this and prefer to put their head in the sand.

In the past, if we had a poor experience with an organization, we would perhaps phone to complain. In our heart of hearts, we knew very little would happen. Organizations are big, individuals are small, and really we know they don't care. The big organizations knew we didn't have any power, and they could spend money telling people how wonderful they were. Granted, if their service was very bad, then prior to the internet eventually word of mouth would spread, but as communications were not fast at that point, this process would take some time. Although nobody likes poor service, most people just put up with it. What else could they do? Enter the Web, and now social media.

Without getting technical, the big difference over the last few years is that instead of just having websites that you need to check to see whether anything has changed, the introduction of RSS feeds has changed the way many people now use the Web. For the uninitiated, an RSS feed enables you to subscribe to the feed through a "reader" – Google Reader, as an example – meaning that you can access this one site and see what is new on all the websites you have subscribed to (Figure 5.1). This has converted the Web from pull to push. We have

---

5 Clay Shirky, How social media can make history (http://www.ted.com/talks/ clay_shirky_how_cellphones_twitter_facebook_can_make_history.html

gone from checking each website, to being told what has changed on each of them.

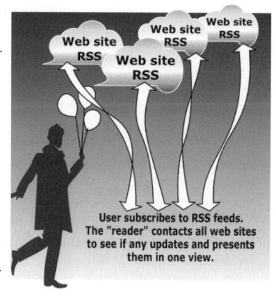

In addition, the use of social media effectively means all of your friends are connected, and their friends are connected, constructing an interlaced network of contacts between people. Both of these features mean that information flows very quickly, and if one person does not pass on a message, someone else

User subscribes to RSS feeds. The "reader" contacts all web sites to see if any updates and presents them in one view.

Figure 5.1 Using RSS feeds

probably will. Some people use Twitter as their stream of "push" information. By following people's messages you can drip in to the real-time stream of data and read the information that people are tweeting about. This is a many-to-many medium. It is these connections that are the key, and the speed is frightening!

As we are moving from the model of mass messages, people are beginning to find expression in the things that make them unique. While Colin likes football for example, which is a mass sport, he also likes old black and white films featuring James Stewart, Humphrey Bogart, and so on, which is more of a minority interest. In the time before social media, if you wanted to participate in one of your specialized interests and meet fellow enthusiasts it was a challenge. How would you find them? For example, let's take an extreme and assume that you are interested in duct tape art, for some reason. Perhaps this is not something that many of you would have considered, but stay with us. How would you find out about this hobby? Before the social media era, you would probably have visited the library and undertaken research to see what you could find. If you found a club you would probably have made contact by writing to it using snail mail, or phoning the organizer. Unless you were very lucky, there probably would not be a great amount of duct tape artwork in close proximity to you, and therefore you would probably have had difficulty in joining a group, or even communicating regularly with fellow enthusiasts. Today's world is very different. We have just Googled "duct tape art," and we had 1,440,000 hits!

What about tea bag cover collecting? Now there is another great hobby! A quick Google reveals 878,000 hits for "tea bag collecting." The top hit is the "Tea bag collection club" (http://teabagsmarcelo. tripod.com/clubteabags.htm):

> The Club goals are:
> To gather every tea bag collector, or collectionist of any other item related to tea like: labels, boxes, cans, tea pots, cups, etc. The idea is to exchange these items, increase and improve the collections, share and make friends with a common interest.

There are clubs of every sort, everywhere. The internet has allowed for specialisms everywhere, and therefore many people now have a long tail of interests. Rather than forcing content ubiquity, the only thing that has become ubiquitous is the Web transportation mechanism. What the Web has done is to create a number of people in small niches, and these people are now connected via social media.

Yes, you've guessed it: there are blogs with people writing about tea bag cover collecting. A quick search directs us to "Tammy's Recipes" (http://www.tammysrecipes.com). Here Tammy shows pictures of how she organizes her collection, and writes about her tea bag covers. She has blogged on her chosen topic, and people have replied from all over the world.

Tammy also Twitters, and has a Facebook page which she refers to on her site. Here at Beyond Philosophy we don't know Tammy at all, but from the look of her blog, Twitter, and Facebook pages, she is a normal mum and has just decided to share recipes. She has found a niche – something she enjoys doing, something she is good at – and she is sharing her experience and expertise in a very open and transparent way. This is social media – a collection of friends and people who have a common interest.

Social media appeal to people in a number of ways. First, the technology provides a great medium to remain in touch with people. Rather than losing touch with friends, you can stay in contact with them. It is an easy way to communicate with many people at once. You can send one invitation when you are having a party and everyone gets it. In my youth we had to send out a physical letter or make individual phone calls to everyone, and people only had landlines, so often they were not there to answer when we called.

Thus, suddenly there are many people whom we can now connect with, however diverse or unusual our hobby is. Therefore, rather than being ubiquitous, the social media are giving us the ability to differentiate and express our personalities. They are shrinking the world and making connections stronger and faster.

This also means that people like Tammy have an outlet for their creativity and passion. Gone are the days where Tammy would have needed millions of dollars for advertising, or a printing press, to get her message out. Now she can establish a blog in a few minutes, for free, and she is communicating with anyone who will listen to her.

This is giving people much more power than they had before. In fact, social media are wrestling power away from organizations. A good example of this is Dave Carroll and his great song "United breaks guitars." In the middle of 2009 Colin was reading Twitter when he saw a buzz around this video. He went on to YouTube and saw the great video that Dave Carroll had released. If you haven't seen it, you must.[6] It tells the story of Dave and his band travelling from Halifax to Nebraska, connecting through Chicago, flying United Airlines. Dave checked in his Taylor guitar (a special, expensive brand of guitar). While on the plane, a passenger saw the ground crew at O'Hara Airport in Chicago throwing the guitar as they loaded the baggage. Dave told the crew, but he felt they could not have cared less. When they arrived at their destination, Dave's worst fears were realized: his guitar was broken. A year of complaining to the airline didn't get any results. We have all been there, haven't we? We feel powerless against the big companies. So Dave decided to take his message to the people via social media, YouTube in this case. He recorded a great song outlining his story. One line in this song sums it up: "I have heard all of your excuses and chased your wild gooses and this attitude of yours I say must go."

As consumers, we all know we are being given the runaround by organizations. We know that when we complain or ask for compensation they put us through many loops in the hope that we will give up and go away. Everyone can relate to the injustice that had befallen Dave, but this time it was not just a few of Dave's friends who were told, the world was told.

When we first saw Dave's video within days of its release, it had registered some 300,000 hits. As of February 2010, it had had 7,624,212 views! We blogged on this at the time, and a quick Google blog search reveals we weren't the only ones. In fact there were 151,767 blog hits on "United breaks guitars"! The story appeared on CNN and other television stations. Times Online[7] estimated that the bad publicity cost United US$180 million in market capitalization and had a massive

---

6   http://www.youtube.com/watch?v=5YGc4zOqozo
7   http://www.timesonline.co.uk/tol/comment/columnists/chris_ayres/
    article6722407.ece

effect on its PR. It must have caused issues internally as well, further lowering employee morale. Also, consider the cost of the staff time involved. Think how many meetings United must have had when the story began to grow. How much senior management time was wasted? Why did all this happen? Because the company didn't do what was right. It had created a culture where its employees and the third parties it employed did not care about customers, and treated their belongings with contempt.

What did United do? Eventually – but only eventually – it did the right thing and gave Dave US$3,000 compensation for the damage to his guitar.[8] Dave, as any true hero would, told them to donate this to charity. This makes the point that for Dave, as for many of us, sagas like this reach a stage where the battle is not about money. It is about justice; it is about respect and self-esteem, a subject we will return to later.

United is living in the old world, not the new. Its staff did not appreciate that there has been a shift of power from organizations to customers. If they had known that damaging Dave's guitar and then failing to compensate him promptly was going to attract this level of coverage, do you think they would have reacted differently? Of course they would. They didn't expect this. Social media are an emerging trend in the Customer Experience, and over the next few years we will see more and more of these cases.

This will lead a number of organizations – but not all – to change the way they deal with customers, and to focus further on their Customer Experience.

As with any change of this nature, it is invariably the senior teams who are lagging behind. Why? Because they are behind the curve technologically. About 58 percent of CEOs are aged between 50 and 59. A quick search reveals that hardly any CEOs of large organizations are tweeting or blogging, and when it seems that they do blog it is often not really the executive blogging, but the PR department.

Senior execs do not "get it."

CEOs might see their kids spending a lot of time on social media, and see the occasional "United breaks guitars" video, but in the main, they think that what happened to United will not happen to them.

---

8   http://www.timesonline.co.uk/tol/comment/columnists/chris_ayres/
    article6722407.ece

They believe they can control the message, as they have done for years. However, they cannot. This tidal wave will swamp everyone.

The only defense is to learn to swim, to move with the tide, and use it to your advantage.

No longer do people need to go to university and get a degree in English to become a journalist. No longer do they need to work their way through regional newspapers to eventually write for the *New York Times*, or the *Financial Times*. Today all you need in order to put across your views is a PC and a connection to the internet. If you talk sense, if you are honest and transparent, if you follow the social media etiquette, and if you can attract readers/followers/friends, you have a platform that can spread your message. This is sending shock waves through the traditional media institutions.

A great example is Glen Tilton, who at the time of writing is the CEO of United Airlines. We did a quick Google and followed a few links, and found a website with the URL http://www.glenntilton.com/. Its home page was headed "Glenn Tilton must go," with the subtitle "United pilots ask for your help in removing an incapable leader."

Would this have happened before the internet? Of course not, as there wasn't a medium to enable this to happen. In theory the disgruntled pilots could have paid for an advert in a newspaper or on the television, but the cost would have been prohibitive. But now, within seconds, a leader can be lampooned, a poor Customer Experience can be discussed, a picture can posted, and millions of people can read it. Scary!

It seems to us that most organizations are scared by social media. They are scared because they can't control it. Jeff Bullas has a great blog (www.jeffbullas.com), and recently listed 28 reasons why CEOs are afraid of social media. How many of these reasons apply to your organization?[9]

1   It is detrimental to employee productivity.
2   It could damage the company's reputation.
3   Security risk.
4   Fear of the unknown.
5   We already have information overload.
6   Don't know enough about it.
7   So much of what's discussed online is shallow and we have real work to do.

---

9   http://jeffbullas.com/2009/08/08/28-reasons-why-the-ceo-is-afraid-of-social-media/

8   We don't have the time or resources to contribute and moderate.
9   Our customers don't use it.
10 Traditional media is still bigger, we will use social media when they are more mainstream.
11 It doesn't fit into current structures.
12 No guaranteed results.
13 The tools to measure and analyze social media aren't mature enough yet.
14 We are in B2B and who wants to hear about our boring product on a blog or Twitter.
15 We will lose control of our brand and image.
16 Upper management won't provide support.
17 Waiting on ROI (return on investment) with facts and figures.
18 We are afraid of making a mistake.
19 Lack of experience.
20 Ignorance.
21 Unwilling to be transparent.
22 Confusion.
23 No money.
24 No expertise.
25 Lack of leadership.
26. Terrified of feedback and truth.
27 The "newness" of it, going to wait.
28 High degree of skepticism.

So there are lots of reasons, but what is the root cause?

We believe the root cause is that people have not yet accepted the need to look at the world in a different way.

You need to accept that the power is shifting, and embrace this. You need to understand that the world is connected, and that this provides a threat, but at the same time a MASSIVE opportunity. You need to be transparent, and realize that this will occasionally cause pain for your organization. You need to invest in this channel, you need to understand that speed is of the essence, and you need to trust your employees to do the right thing.

Barry Judge, Chief Marketing Officer for Best Buy, is a good example of someone who sees these things and who is doing something about it. First, Barry has his own blog, www.barryjudge.com. He twitters as well: http://twitter.com/BestBuyCMO. In addition he has started a number of social media initiatives at Best Buy. We'll let Barry tell you his views on social media:

I am fascinated with social media, its impacts on the marketing profession, our culture overall and the way I do my job. I am aware that most people are still learning about social media. For example, I was at a dinner with 15 fellow CMOs from other companies recently. In an informal poll around the table only two of my counterparts used Twitter or Facebook. Another example: a while ago I was at a meeting and talking about Twitter, and one of my colleagues asked me if I had invented the word!

Social media are extremely interesting for a variety of reasons. I strongly believe in the idea of "crowd sourcing," getting a number of people to input to an idea. Also I believe in "co-creation," working with customers, employees, and others to devise the best solution. I know that I don't have the best ideas myself, and that the 5,000 smartest people do not work at Best Buy corporate, or any one place for that matter. Through social media it is possible to dramatically increase the "intellect and passion" working on things that I care about.

Another example comes from Steve Sickel, Senior Vice President, Distribution and Relationship Marketing. IHG. IHG is a hotel group which owns the brands Holiday Inn, Intercontinental, Crown Plaza, Staybridge, Candelwood, and Hotel Indigo. Steve's view is:

Part of the trick for us in using our online communities is to get the communities to help us do our jobs. There are many people out there who want to be our brand advocates. They want to shout the message about our brands from the rooftops! The trick is to create a win/win that enables us to harness this so the customer gets something out of it, and we get our message spread far and wide by someone who, frankly, has much more credibility (i.e. a customer) than a big corporate message or campaign.

I think, like everyone, we have one foot in the water on this one and the other one out, and we're sorting things out gradually.

These are just two examples of companies that are embracing the change. In some organizations we are witnessing a revolution. These are the organizations that are quickly embracing this new channel, and this is giving them a competitive advantage, but these organizations are in the minority. Most organizations are evolving. Here is Steve Sickel, IHG, again.

We have a business objective we are trying to achieve, and that's the way we approach our social marketing agenda. I think a lot of companies miss this and just jump on the bandwagon because they think they need to be involved with social marketing, but they don't really know why. This is a recipe for disaster. We have a very practical approach to our social marketing agenda. We want to drive a business outcome – delivering incremental revenue into our hotels by engaging with our customers so that they shop with us more than the others we're racing against.

Our research demonstrates the evolutionary that path organizations are on: see Figure 5.2.

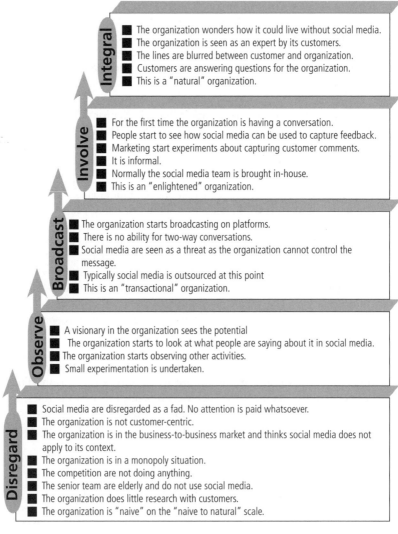

Figure 5.2 Social media engagement stages of maturity

What stage of maturity is your organization at? What are you doing to move it forward?

A good example of the stages of maturity is Delta Airlines. As our US office is based in Atlanta we tend to use Delta Airlines. Colin is a Gold Card member and has become a "fan" of Delta on Facebook. At time of writing Delta had 13,831 fans on Facebook. There are lots and lots of comments from fans about the good and bad things they see when using Delta, but there is no comment from Delta itself. So we contacted Delta to ask why they are not responding to the comments. Here is an extract from their reply:

> We are fairly new to the social space, having a full time position as social media manager just since October. While there are several pages out there claiming to be Delta, we currently do not have an active Facebook page. That will be launched in the next month or so. We want to ensure we have a great customer experience when you interact with the brand and therefore are taking a careful and measured approach to all our communication channels.

This is a prime example of a company in the early stages of its social media presence. Another example is Aflac, which is one of the best brands in the United States. (Readers elsewhere might like to know that it sells supplementary health insurance.) Aflac's primary markets are the United States and Japan. A key image used in its branding is a duck, and the Aflac duck has become well known and loved throughout America. We are proud to have been working with Aflac for a number of years. Laree Daniel, the Senior Vice President of Customer Assurance Organization, explains the reason that Aflac is operating in the social media space:

> Just as a shopper will choose to shop online, at brick-and-mortar, or a combination thereof, marketing interactions are most often a combination of channels, each with their own strengths, weaknesses, and norms. To maintain our strong brand and make the most of the social media opportunity, it is essential that we understand this fact and act accordingly to ensure our presence exists in each of these channels, including social.
>
> People are spending a greater share of their time as consumers of social media, creating opportunities to evangelize for their favorite brands among their own networks. We have a choice. Aflac can tell people that our product is great, however it is far more effective if Marge from Utah, who plays softball and is a respected member of her community, tells her network that Aflac is great, without any prompting from us. We focus on trying to provide a great Customer Experience. We want our customers to share their opinions and experiences of Aflac within their own circles of friends. We

know this generates favorable results. In addition we use their opinions and feedback in product creation and development of service delivery.

Social media is not just about use with customers. A new breed of managers are using them as a very powerful tool to communicate internally. Darren Cornish is another client, whom we first worked with when he was Director (VP) of Customer Experience at one of the largest insurance companies in the United Kingdom. We'll let Darren take up the story of how he used social media internally to help effect change.

I wanted a way to connect with people across the organization, communicate to them openly and honestly about the problems we faced and what we are doing about them as part of the plan to galvanize people into action. I decided to set up an internal blog. On a regular basis I posted examples of good and bad experiences with our company and from my personal life as a consumer myself. This blog grew to be the most popular page on the intranet, in fact more people visited this than they did the CEO page!

At first, the company were nervous about some of the comments people would write – as you can imagine some of them were not complimentary. To the company's credit, they decided not to intervene. I argued this was becoming part of the agent of positive change for them. The blog was a way of saying "It's OK to talk about this," "It's OK to raise things that go wrong."

I used this to explain what was happening to improve the Customer Experience. A number of my colleagues were worried that it would take too long for things to change and more negative comments would follow. But we didn't find that. We found if you are honest with people, if you tell them the truth, they are not stupid. They know that things take time.

Within two years the internal blog was receiving over 3,000 visits a day (from the company's total staff of 9,000) and over 150 comments! Service issues surfaced online, and other readers came forward with ways of solving the problems. Front-line contact centre people were assisted by Finance in building business cases and by IT in gaining prioritized actions. On one particular morning the CEO himself joined in the commenting. Bearing in mind I was working for an English company, the very next comment was, "Wow, who's next to contribute, the Queen?"

I use the blog to "shine a light" on service heroes in the business. The blog connected all employees to the "higher purpose" of whatever job they were doing – that of providing peace of mind to their customers and being there for them in moments of crisis. Many people away from the front line commented that they had "forgotten" that was what their company really did. The blog helped give their roles meaning again.

The service improvements we implemented positively affected over 2 million customers and removed hundreds of thousands of pounds of cost from the business. Our people across the company scored the annual employee survey question, "I believe my company is customer focused" 22 percent higher in the year after the blog gathered its large audience.

I would highly commend this as part of an effective Customer Experience program.

As you can see, social media are not just an external phenomenon. As Darren outlines, they can play an important role in the organization's internal culture as well. This needs a change of mindset, it needs to be embraced to get the best results, but we hope you can start to see the potential. However you will only see that potential if you embrace the fact that customers and employees are people, and people are emotional animals who are driven by emotions and basic needs.

Social media are changing everything and at the same time they are changing nothing.

They change nothing, because fundamentally social media are addressing a very basic human need. We humans are social animals. We know we need to look at our customers through "experience psychology" eyes. As such, no conversation would be complete without looking at one of the cornerstones of psychology, Maslow's hierarchy of needs. A number of you will have heard about this, but we intend to go into the all-important detail to ensure that you understand its effect on social media. In the process you will be able to look through what is happening today, and project yourself into the future of where this is going, independent of the platforms.

Maslow's work was launched in 1943. He called it the theory of human motivation.[10] His hierarchy breaks down into the following areas.

Physiological needs

As Maslow told us,[11] our first need is a physiological one, the need for food, water, sleep, sex and so on. These are the basics of life.

Safety needs

The need for safety is a big driver for anyone. In our last book, *The DNA of Customer Experience: How emotions drive value*, we conducted two years of research, which was independently vetted by the London

---

10 http://psychclassics.yorku.ca/Maslow/motivation.htm
11 http://en.wikipedia.org/wiki/Maslow's_hierarchy_of_needs

Business School, and discovered the 20 emotions that drive and destroy value (see page 34). "Safe" was one of the 20 emotions. This means we can prove statistically that the need for safety drives or destroys value. Value can be determined in many ways, but typically our clients use revenue, brand, customer satisfaction, net promoter, and customer retention as their descriptors of value. We can show the revenue increase or decrease from evoking any of the 20 emotions. Therefore, when looking at your social media experience we can identify the touch points or attributes of a Customer Experience that drive and destroy value.

A common example is that people need to be confident their information will not be used inappropriately. If they are revealing lots of personal details it needs to be done in a safe environment. Therefore, the brand or platform they are using must reinforce this and provide adequate coverage. This is why there has been a great debate about how Facebook and other social networking sites should use the information that people place on the site. For example, if someone writes on their Facebook page about their upcoming wedding, would it be acceptable for Facebook to start placing advertisements about weddings on their page? The general agreement is that it would be inappropriate to do this without the user's permission. This is an example of a practice that would start to destroy value. As another example, people needs to be confident that their data is safe from being accessed by hackers.

To feel safe, people like predictability. They know what is going to happen and when, therefore they feel safe. If you change the style of your home page every week, people will feel unsure when and if any change is going to happen, and this can result in their not feeling safe. For example, every time Facebook changes its home page, groups form to protest against the changes. People find it unexpected and want to go to the old design, even though each change essentially improves the ease of use.

For someone to feel safe they need to trust circumstances and people. Again, from the research for our last book, we know that "trust" is one of the emotions that drives or destroys value. Trust has also become a key issue for many organizations recently. People know that many organizations are economical with the truth. It is not that they actually lie (although some do), but they might avoid telling customers something that, if the customer knew and acted on it, would prevent them from maximizing their profit. For example, there might be a product or service that would better suit a customer's needs but doesn't provide the company with as much revenue. To fail to tell the customer about this opportunity is something that affects the trust in the customer relationship.

Trust is a key driver in the social media experience. Social media create the opportunity for an organization to build trust with a customer. They also provide an opportunity for them to show that they are economical with the truth. The key is to be transparent. If things are transparent, then people trust them.

Who are the people you trust? Your family and friends are a good start. If you want an opinion about what car to buy, do you go to a friend who is knowledgeable about cars, or do your visit a local garage and speak to the salesperson? We are sure most of you would talk with a friend. You know that the garage will be biased and will not have your best interests so much at heart. Enter social media. Now your "friends" group is wider, and it is easier and faster to contact them, so you can, for instance, tell your social media network that you're looking at buying a car, and ask for their advice.

Nielsen research[12] reveals that 90 percent of consumers trust recommendations from people they know. Seventy percent of people prefer using sites like TripAdvisor.com, where the public can write in their own words what they think of a product or service (on this site, a hotel, for example) on the basis of their own experience, to company-owned sites that only say what the company wants to say. Independent feedback has shown us that vacation companies do not always give an unbiased view of what they offer. For example, they tend to suggest that rooms and pools are larger than they really are by using wide-angle lens. Tripadvisor.com and similar sites have become so popular now that some vacation companies have allowed customers to put their views in brochures. Amazon now puts customer reviews on its sites. It knows that customers trust the opinion of other customers more than that of someone who has a vested interest.

Within this part of Maslow's hierarchy of needs comes "financial security." Feeling safe means that you have enough money to buy food, which is part of the physiological needs.

Again, it's important to recognize how people's needs are manifesting themselves in the social media experience. To help gain financial security people need to make money. This is done through having a job or by having your own company and gaining clients. To do this you need to network and make contacts. Thus, social media are full of people wanting to network. Now, let us be clear: we are not saying this is bad. All we are doing is pointing out the root causes for people getting involved. How people decide to network and how overt they are in their real aims is a different issue. You will see other reasons why people want to network later.

---

12 http://blog.nielsen.com/nielsenwire/consumer/global-advertising-consumers-trust-real-friends-and-virtual-strangers-the-most/

Social needs

As we have learned through experience psychology, people are social animals. There is nothing better than having a good time with family and friends, a barbecue with the family, going down the local restaurant with friends, house parties, and other gatherings. For example, Colin goes to football (soccer) with his father and daughter Coralie to see Luton Town FC. He enjoys the soccer, but important too is the sense of belonging. It's about the people who sit around him, and it's about identifying with a team. It's even about supporting an unfashionable team, and accepting that Luton are usually the underdogs. It's about belonging to a community. It's about a tribe.

We need partners and friends; hence we join groups and clubs. This is why the worst punishment a person can get in prison is solitary confinement.

Tribes come in many forms. We have already described some tribes, such as the tea bag cover collector tribe and the duct tape art tribe.

It is easier to stay in touch with more people using social media than it is to send everyone individual emails or phone them individually. Even by simply sending a text message you feel a connection with a person, and this can help you to not feel lonely.

An anthropologist, Richard Dunbar, has famously worked out that the average number of people that we actually have a relationship with is 148, which is commonly rounded to 150. This is now known as the Dunbar number. We know some people who claim to have over 1,000 "friends," but Dunbar would dispute whether the brain can deal with that number of friendships, and actually have a meaningful relationship with all those people. Are these true friends? Muhammad Ali famously said that he believed you would be very lucky if you had five true friends in a lifetime. We believe the Dunbar number is a good guide. What is meant by the word "friend" or "follower" in social media language? In essence, it is a contact, someone who is part of your social group or groups. Thus "friends" can be quite tenuous.

Esteem needs

Looking further at Tammy's case, we are sure that because of her knowledge of her subject and the number of visits she gets to her blog, she feels accepted and respected. In fact you can see that this is the case by reading people's posts on her blog and noticing the tone of them. As a result she must – rightly – feel very satisfied. Being accepted is an important part of being in a tribe. In fact, to be in a tribe you must be accepted. Once you have achieved this, you look for respect. In the movies you can often hear gangsters saying "He disrespected me." The need for respect is a very powerful motivator, and nowhere is this more true than in the social media experience.

When someone "follows" you or asks you to join your group, by definition you have been accepted, otherwise they would not have asked to join. Respect can be gained by being someone in authority, a "go-to guy," the person who is knowledgeable about a subject. If you want to find out about tea bag covers then Tammy is your woman. People no longer need academic qualifications to achieve respect or be an authority on a subject.

Maslow also talks about confidence in the part of his work on human motivators. Respect and acceptance then build confidence. When you feel confident in social media you feel you have a voice. People post things on other people's blogs. They comment on what is happening in their environment. Finally, this demonstrates people feeling valued. Again, "valued" is one of the emotions that can drive and destroy value. To make people feel valued in the social media experience, the best bloggers will acknowledge their input to the blog. Therefore, people do not feel valued when they ask a question over social media that is subsequently not replied to.

Many of us are guilty of setting up Facebook or Twitter sites and frequently monitoring how many followers or friends we have. The more we get, the better we feel. Why? Because we are social animals, and because it is an indication of being accepted and respected, as well as our opinion being valued.

Self-actualization

Finally, we have self-actualization – the need to maximize one's own potential. Self-actualization can be about helping others; it is about values, not about monetary success.

We need to feel our life has been worthwhile. In fact, 72 percent of bloggers are hobbyists and blog for fun, and 76 percent do it to "express themselves."[13]

Many people share information not for financial gain as we indicated in the safety needs, but because it makes them feel worthwhile and it gives them pleasure to help others. For example Comcast, a cable company in the United States, has people monitoring the twitter-sphere (that is, people who use Twitter) to pick up on people who have complaints.[14] It has found that some of its customers have been trying to help other customers. A recent *Business Week* interview reported:

---

13 http://www.techcrunch.com/2009/10/16/2009-state-of-the-blogosphere-the-full-blogworld-presentation/

14 http://www.businessweek.com/managing/content/jan2009/ca20090113_373506_page_3.htm.

Thanks to the friendly Twitter network Frank has built up, customers occasionally help one another, as he discovered a few weeks earlier when he mentioned in a Tweet that he had an important family event during the day and would be unavailable. Once the event ended that evening, he logged onto Twitter at home to see which customers in the Twitt-o-sphere needed help that day.

"I found that people who didn't work for Comcast were responding, saying: 'Let Frank have his day. Can I help?'" he recalls. "They were saying: 'Here, try this.' And it was the most amazing thing. That day I understood the effectiveness of what we do."

Another example is writing a post on Tripadvisor about your vacation experience, which can be seen as a form of self-actualization. You are not doing it for your own benefit, you are doing it for the good of others, and when we talk about others we start to discuss the word "community."

We are certain that you will have heard that social media are about establishing a community. What does community actually mean? In a seminal 1986 study, McMillan and Chavis[15] identified four elements of engendering a "sense of community":

- membership
- influence
- integration and fulfillment of needs
- shared emotional connection.

To create a sense of community, people need to see themselves as members of that community. As members we want to have some influence, we want our voice to be heard. As part of a community we want to feel integrated, a part of something, as we have seen with Maslow's hierarchy of needs. People want to share an emotional connection. People want to share common emotions. Think of sports audiences that share the emotional highs and lows.

To round off this chapter let us refer back to the preceding chapters and remind you of the concept of experience psychology. This helps us to offer the following definition of what we would like to see as a "social media experience." Everyone talks about social media, but this for us this puts too much emphasis on the word "media," and not enough on the experience.

---

15 D. W. McMillan and D. M. Chavis (1986) "Sense of community: a definition and theory," *Journal of Community Psychology*, 14(1), pp. 6–23.

Digital social media experience definition:
A technology-enabled social interaction that helps to meet psychological needs: safety, belonging, esteem and self-actualization, and the resultant emotions evoked. Technology enables a wider, faster, more frequent engagement between people, and thus creates a digital social media experience.

As you can imagine this was not done without other people's input, and following the best uses of social media we put draft of this definition out to people on our blog and via Twitter. Our thanks go to the following contacts for their contributions. Check them out: they are all fellow enthusiasts.

Twitter	**Website**
http://twitter.com/Futurescape	http://www.futurescape.in
http://twitter.com/BobThompson	www.Customerthink.com
http://twitter.com/patgibbons	www.Codebaby.com
http://twitter.com/pbultema	http://beingguy1067.wordpress.com
http://twitter.com/guy1067 –	

6 The human social media experience

Blurring the links between customer service and marketing

Twelpforce is a great example of how social media have the ability to change the way we do business and enhance the Customer Experience. Barry Judge, Chief Marketing Officer of Best Buy, talks about Twelpforce and its innovative use of Twitter:

> Twelpforce is a service that enlists the passion and knowledge of Best Buy's vast employee base to bring assistance directly to customers via the micro blogging site, Twitter. How it works is quite simple. When a customer has a question about a product or service or even has a customer service issue, all they need to do is tweet this over Twitter. This is then picked up by one of our Best Buy employees from across all operations, including Blue Shirts who are in-store and Geek Squad. They then answer the question from wherever they are. From the customer's perspective it works well, all from the comfort of their keyboard or mobile phone. Twelpforce is a new resource for our customers to help them do the things they aspire to do with technology. To the extent we are able to help, I believe these efforts will build trust with customers and improve their experience.
>
> In addition to customer benefits, I also think Twelpforce can be a catalyst to help us to think very differently about customer service across our company. No longer do we need to passively wait for customers to come to us. With Twelpforce specifically, and social media in general, we can actively seek out the conversations that increasingly are happening outside our channels. I also think this initiative can change our definition of customer service. No longer is customer service a department, but something that all of us can do. In my view, Twelpforce begins to really blur the lines between customer service and more traditional one-way marketing communications.
>
> Finally, this idea raises the visibility and participation of social media in our field teams. Culturally this is a very good thing as we think about how to

connect better with our local communities. Few media can be as local and personal as social media.

Finally, Twelpforce is obviously an experiment. Indeed, it is a very public one as we have placed ads on TV showing how customers can use it. With this publicity comes a certain amount of risk. We are OK with that. The positives outweigh the negatives.

On our journey to improve our customer experience, I know we will make mistakes. Heck, I have made many mistakes in my own use of social media. However, I also know we will learn from them and be a smarter company, and through making mistakes we will better serve our customers going forward.

In our view, Barry and Best Buy should be applauded. They are pushing the boundaries of how to use a social media experience to enhance the Customer Experience. They are willing to take a risk. All too often, we see organizations that are paralyzed by the fear of failure. Well done, Best Buy, whether it succeeds or fails.

All good initiatives typically start with research about what customers want or need. The good news is that we have worked with www.CustomerThink.com and Bob Thompson to undertake this research for you. We have learned to dig below the surface and find out what the customer wants and needs, as well driving value for your organization, and to do this it is imperative we use some of our specialized psychological techniques, which were outlined in the previous chapters. Normal research will not give you the richness of data that you need to be successful.

Therefore, so that you can understand the methodology we will quickly outline how we go about this, first to enable you to make more sense of the results, and second, to act as a practical demonstration of how to go about this type of research.

To begin with we segmented the social media experience into three main segments:

- **Personal social media experiences:** People who use the media to stay in touch with friends and family on sites like Facebook, sharing photos on flickr, uploading videos of family vacations on YouTube, and so on.
- **Customer social media experiences:** People who use social media to seek advice before purchasing a product or service. This could be visiting TripAdvisor to get an idea of places to go on holiday, visiting a company's websites to research televisions, or reading Amazon recommendation lists. Being a fan on Facebook of a company is another example.
- **Business social media experiences:** This is when you are using social media in the business setting. It could be that you want to keep up to date on what is happening in your industry and are

reading blogs. It could be expanding your business knowledge or writing a blog in the business context, or status updates on Twitter, Linked in, and so on.

Table 6.1 The top seven attributes based on their desirability

Overall	Personal	Business	Customer
The helpfulness of links posted by other people	The use of pictures	The helpfulness of links posted by other people	Other people's comments
The ease of use of social media	The extent to which the content is entertaining	The quality of the information I come across	The helpfulness of links posted by other people
The speed of finding relevant information	The helpfulness of links posted by other people	The speed of finding relevant information	The quality of the information I come across
The quality of the information I come across	The ease of use of social media	The ability to send direct messages to others	The creative ideas I come across
The ability to send direct messages to others	The ability to make new friends/contacts	The ease of use of social media	The ease of use of social media
The creative ideas I come across	The ability to send direct messages to others	The creative ideas I come across	The speed of finding relevant information
The ability to make new friends/contacts	The speed of finding relevant information	Other people's comments	Trustworthiness of the information

The seven lowest attributes based on their desirability

Overall	Personal	Business	Customer
The feeling that I am accepted	The feeling that I am accepted	The feeling that I am accepted	The availability of a 3G signal
The sense of esteem I get	The sense of esteem I get	The sense of esteem I get	The feeling that I am important
The feeling that I am important	The feeling that I am important	The availability of a 3G signal	The sense of esteem I get
The availability of a 3G signal	The clarity of the texts	The feeling that I am important	The feeling that I am accepted
The respect I get from others	The respect I get from others	The respect I get from others	The respect I get from others
The clarity of the texts	The availability of a 3G signal	Security of the media	Level of encouragement I receive to post my comments and express my opinion
Safety of the environment	Security of the media	Clarity of the texts	Safety of the environment

The next step was to "crowd source" (put out on social media for lots of people to comment and give their views) a list of what makes up a social media experience. We call these the attributes of an experience. You will see a list of them in Table 6.1. These numbered some 40 different attributes per customer segment. As readers of our previous books will know, we then looked at this research from three aspects: the rational or physical side of the experience, the emotional side, and subconscious aspects of the social media experience.

Here are some examples of the "rational" parts of a social media experience:

■ people referring to your comments on their blog
■ the speed of accessing information
■ the ease of using the social media
■ the quality of the information
■ the page layout/design of social media sites.

We also investigated the "emotional" side of the social media experience. Some examples include:

■ feeling that I am important when using social media
■ feeling that I am accepted when using social media
■ the respect I get from others when using social media
■ the sense of esteem I get when using social media
■ the trustworthiness of the information when using social media.

To recap, we now have everything we want. We know the segments of customers we are researching and we know what attributes of the social experience we are going to ask them about. Now to conduct the research. We then conducted the research over the phone or via customer panels online.

Table 6.1 lists the top seven most desired and least desired attributes of a social media experience, segmented by personal, business, and customer social media experiences and overall.

As you see from these results, people say that the most important and desirable attributes are mainly rational. The least desired attributes fall on the emotional side of the experience. This indicates that we should not focus on making people feel accepted, important, or any of Maslow's hierarchy of needs. This research tells us the main attributes that people want in a social media experience are:

■ the ease of social media
■ the speed of finding the relevant information
■ the helpfulness of links posted by other people.

Consequently, if you want to start taking advantage of the emerging trend of social media experiences, focus on these areas of desirability. After all, the internet is just a logical system and the experience is an entirely rational one, isn't it?

WRONG!

This is a great example of what many organizations do wrong. They ask customers what they want, and they do not look into the psychological aspects of the person and test the answers they get. If you ask customers what they want they will tell you. Alternatively, to put it in a more accurate way, they will tell you what they think they want. However, is this what customers really want? Could it not be that sometimes they are not able to articulate what is really driving their actions, emotions, and desires? Is it that they have not considered the deeper psychological needs and their deep-rooted motivations for engaging with social media in the first place?

This is the problem with many research methodologies today. As you will have read in the previous chapters, to get to true customer insights, it is essential to understand experience psychology and adopt the methods of research we have already written about. Customers do not always know what they want!

As we have said, we always use the analogy of an onion. We have to peel back the onion to see what is in the layers below.

Take the example above of Twelpforce. How many of you said, "I know what I want is to be able to send a tweet into Best Buy for someone to answer my question." Sometimes customers do not know what they want, or cannot articulate it. It this therefore critical to use psychological techniques to dig into what customers want.

This piece of research demonstrates that we have only looked superficially at customer requirements at this point. A much deeper understanding needs to be sought. Maybe the person undertaking the research recalled that they saw some pictures on Facebook the previous evening, and answered, "I like the use of pictures." Let us be clear, we are not saying these things are unimportant. We are saying that you need to be very certain of what customers want before you start changing or building your Customer Experience if you don't want to waste a lot of time, effort, and money.

So what have we learned from this?

■ It is critical to use experience psychological research techniques to look through the layers of the onion of what is truly driving customers.

■ To peel back the layers of the onion calls for a deep understanding of psychology and people to be able to determine what is really happening.

■ It then needs sophisticated, statistical methodologies to ensure that the answers are statistically accurate, to enable a social media experience strategy to be built on firm ground.

Let's make it very clear: the research discussed above only tells us what customers think they want at a very superficial level. It is incomplete and just the tip of the iceberg. The big danger is that it will lead you to take action on attributes that are not as important as others. While it is a genuine piece of research, it is only illustrative of how organizations can get it so wrong and waste time, money, and effort on things that are not important.

What do customers want, then, if not this list above? In addition, another critical aspect that we have not addressed is what drives value for your organization. It's OK finding out what customers want, but you also need to ask yourself, will providing it to them result in a profit? In our experience, this is a key question that senior executives will want clarity on.

Let's go back to Steve Sickel, Senior Vice President, Distribution and Relationship Marketing from IHG, who provides some wise words on the focus on proving value to the organization.

> Ultimately this stuff works. It is important not to lose sight that we're in the business of creating business. We approach social media in that same way. We pursue a social marketing agenda to drive business. We're not a charity and we're not engaging in social marketing just because it's interesting. We do it because it's profitable. If it was just interesting and it didn't drive our business results then I would have wasted time, money, and effort on something that didn't have a payback, and I can't afford to waste time, money, and effort.

To find out what customers really want and what drives value, we have used one of our experience psychology techniques, the Emotional Signature we discussed earlier. To recap, following two years of research vetted by London Business School we discovered the emotions that drive and destroy value. You will see from Figure 6.1 that these 20 emotions can be sorted into four clusters.

This was a piece of breakthrough research.

It is important that you understand what these emotions mean and how they manifest themselves in a social media experience. Table 6.2 outlines this for you.

93

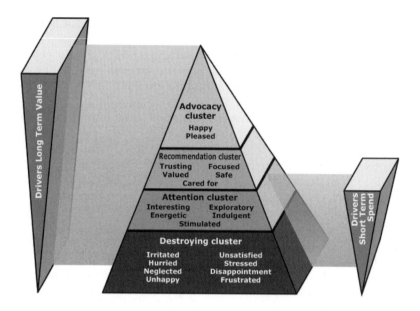

Figure 6.1 The hierarchy of emotional value

Now for the final bit of the jigsaw. For the very first time the Emotional Signature® enables you to statistically prove a link between evoking an emotion and generating an increase or decrease in "value." Examples of value in this sense are a revenue increase, an increase in customer satisfaction, net promoter score, brand value, customer retention, customer loyalty, customer acquisition, or other specified customized requirements.

> **Our objective in undertaking an Emotional Signature® for the social media experience was to establish what drives or destroys value for personal, business, and customer social media experiences.**

To be clear, we want to know, for example, whether if we increased "the use of pictures," it would drive more value than increasing the "feeling of importance the customer gets" from a social experience. When we know the answer to this, we then know how to design an experience.

Our first step was to determine what we mean by value, as this can mean different things to different people. Again we "crowd sourced" and discussed this with people in the industry. As a result we devised the value indicators listed on page 97.

Table 6.2 Emotions that drive and destroy value applied to social media

Cluster/ emotion	Meaning and example
Destroying cluster	
Hurried	Meaning: The feeling of being pressurized.
	Examples: This can happen with social media because of the speed that things work at. Everything is in real time. People expect an instant reply, therefore someone can feel hurried when they would prefer to reflect on things. Another way this could manifest itself is the need to stay in contact with people, which applies social pressure to do things, respond to requests or a simple blog post.
Neglected	Meaning: If you feel neglected, people are not paying attention to you. For example, you send a friend request and the person ignores you. You send a direct message over Twitter and the person doesn't reply.
	Examples: You can feel neglected when you send a direct message to someone who is ignoring you. It could be that you have set up a group and haven't invited one person.
Unhappy	Meaning: If you are unhappy, this tends to be an overarching feeling and could be caused by the consolidation of other feelings.
	Examples: You could be unhappy because you are feeling neglected, for example. In social media, the same is true. You could feel unhappy because your messages are being ignored and you haven't been invited to join a group.
Stressed	Meaning: The feeling of too much to do in a short space of time.
	Examples: You have too many things to do, such as update your status, reply to direct messages, write a blog, catch up on reading blogs. Perhaps you are spending so much time on Facebook that you are not getting anything else done. You might be worrying about something that someone has said about you on social media. You could feel stressed after someone has written a post arguing that you don't know what you are talking about.
Irritated	Meaning: This is the feeling of being constantly annoyed with someone or something. An irritation can be small but really annoys you!
	Examples: The way that people reply to all in Twitter and you can only see half a conversation; the sales-focused group emails that you get on occasions.
Disappointed	Meaning: The feeling of disappointment is when you have been let down.
	Examples: You might feel disappointed at the speed of the media, or disappointed that Twitter is over capacity, or disappointed that someone has used your materials and hasn't acknowledged you.

Table 6.2 continued

Frustrated	Meaning: The feeling of wanting to do something but being unable to for one reason or another.
	Examples: The log-in of a site; the poor layout of a site that makes you spends lots of time looking for the right page; being frustrated that a group leader will not let you join a group you'd like to be part of.
Dissatisfied	Meaning: The feeling of not getting what you expect. The opposite to feeling satisfied.
	Examples: You might be dissatisfied with the fact that your post has not been approved by the moderator, or by the recommendations of contacts you have been provided with.
Attention cluster	
Exploring	Meaning: The feeling you get when you enjoy investigating or discovering something. This is the feeling you get when you are exploring something; maybe on vacation visiting a new town, or looking for books in a bookshop.
	Examples: In the social media context, exploring new articles, or reading new content on Twitter or another site. Looking for new people to follow, or looking for reviews of products to buy.
Interested	Meaning: The feeling of being absorbed in a subject.
	Example: In social media you feel interested in what you are reading, what the blogs say. People's comments on a subject that interests you.
Indulgent	Meaning: The feeling of doing something that is purely for your enjoyment.
	Example: In social media, you might be spending a large amount of time "talking" with your friends, something that you would not normally do when you know you have other things to do. Reading up on a vacation that you are planning to take.
Energized	Meaning: When you are feeling energized you are enthusiastic, buzzed.
	Example: In social media, you could have read something that excites you. You might have seen someone refer to your work and give it a great review. You could have found the solution to a problem.
Stimulated	Meaning: When you feel stimulated you feel aroused to take action. Potentially the beginning of being energized.
	Example: You can be stimulated by a creative article you have read, or the review of a product you have investigated.

Table 6.2 continued

Recom-mendation cluster	
Focused	Meaning: The feeling of being focused is not a normal emotion people talk about.
	Example: The feeling of focused is when you are very absorbed by a subject. Perhaps you are watching a movie and you start to cry as you are fully focused on the film, fully absorbed. In social media you might be engrossed in the materials that are available, or fully engaged in the conversations over Twitter,.
Safe	Meaning: The feeling of safety is that you trust the environment, feeling secure.
	Example: In social media your account will not be hacked. Your information is safe and not being used by someone else.
Cared for	Meaning: When you feel cared for you feel someone is looking after you.
	Example: In social media this could be receiving messages; having a "chat." Someone is looking out for your interests. Being supported in comments that are being made against you. The acknowledgement of your return and thanks of posting another comment on the blog.
Valued	Meaning: You feel valued when your importance is acknowledged in word or deed.
	Example: You feel valued when people retweet your tweets. When people quote you in their blogs - assuming it is positive! When people recommend your blog to others. Where the bloggers refer to you.
Trust	Meaning: The feeling of security, safety.
	Example: You feel you can trust someone when they do what they say. They do not plagiarize your material, they are transparent and honest.
Advocacy cluster	
Pleased	Meaning: Pleased is an output emotion. When you are pleased you feel mildly happy and contented.
	Example: You feel pleased because you feel valued and cared for.
Happy	Meaning: Happy is the same as pleased in the sense that is an output emotion again. You feel happy because of all the other things that happened.
	You might be happy with your social media experience, or happy with the blogs you read.

Value indicators

We wanted to see how social media experiences are perceived. Are they trusted? Do they satisfy people's expectations? How preferred they are? Then we could try to establish the result of that, in terms of for example loyalty or retention. In each of the three segments, we defined these as value indicators:

- the level of trust in social media
- customer loyalty
- net promoter score
- customer retention
- satisfied with the use of social media
- being the preferred means of communication.

To demonstrate that a social media experience touches a person's deepest inner nature, we used some of the work from Maslow's hierarchy of needs to translate people's behavior. Additionally, in order to take into account the emotional side and how this links to Maslow's hierarchy of needs, we set the following as value indicators:

- Social media make me feel like I belong to a community.
- Social media make me feel respected.
- Social media make me feel connected to other people.
- Social media are a trustworthy source of information.
- Social media are a safe channel of communication.

So now we have the attributes we outlined above of the Customer Experience, we have the value indicators, and finally we need to measure these against customer emotions. To do this we used the research from our last book, *The DNA of Customer Experience: How emotions drive and destroy value*, and the research with the London Business School. At this point, we put the parts together and undertook some advanced statistical analysis.

What we discovered in our experience psychology research

First, and most importantly, we discovered that people's social media experiences are absolutely driven by emotion. We discovered that Maslow's theories live well in the social media experience. Aspects of Maslow's hierarchy of need – for example esteem and acceptance – are important, and others were statistically confirmed as forming a major part of the social media experience. This, then, is directly opposite to the first piece of research illustrated above.

We also discovered that personal and business social media experiences are much more aligned than customer social media experiences. When you think about this, it makes sense. In the personal and business social media experiences, there are a number of aspects in common. Critically, they are both concerned with communications: with the personal social media experience it is communications with friends and family, whereas with the business social media experience it is "contacts." In both contexts people use social media to stay in touch. Business people want to stay in touch with customers, colleagues, and people they think can help them in some way. As we all know, in the business world we call this "networking," but in essence, a few layers into the onion, it is the same thing as staying in touch with family and friends. Customer social media experiences are more concerned with information, not meeting and connecting with people.

As part of an Emotional Signature®, we always produce what we call an emotional profile (see Figure 6.2 for a sample). This shows how customers are feeling towards your organization, or their level of emotional engagement. We will be illustrating one of these for each of personal, business, and customer experiences, so they are worthy of explanation. In Figure 6.2 we see the results for "overall social media:" that is, personal, business, and customers combined. Along the horizontal axis are the emotions that drive or destroy value. The vertical line shows how strongly these emotions are felt (or not felt). It is important to remember that you are trying to get the attention, recommendation, and advocacy cluster emotions up as high as you can, while trying to get the destroying cluster down as low as you can.

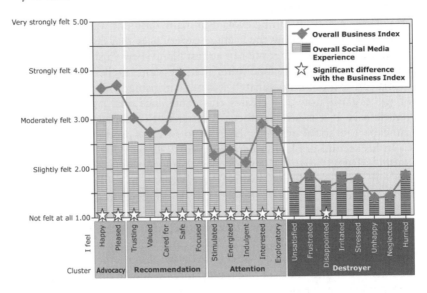

Figure 6.2 Emotional profile: overall social media experience

The "overall Business index" line is drawn from the material in our last book, *The DNA of Customer Experience: How emotions drive value.* In other words, it summarizes all the research we conducted. That research was not specific to social media experiences, but instead looked at all different types of customer experience, both business to consumer and business to business, on both sides of the Atlantic, using different channels: shops, online, face to face experiences, over the phone, and so on. Therefore, we can compare the social media experience with an "average" customer experience.

Finally, the stars indicate that there is a statistically significant difference between the overall social media results and the overall business index. It is not always easy to tell visually when the differences are significant, so this is very useful information.

So what does this tell us? First, in the Destroying cluster of emotions we see the "business index" or "average" experience compared with the "overall social media experience." It appears they follow a very similar pattern. We can also see that the Attention cluster of emotions (interested, energized, exploratory, indulgent, and stimulated) is performing a lot better than any of the other clusters. This is probably because social media are still quite new, so they evoke these emotions. For example, if you come across a new blog that is covering a topic you are interested in, and whose writer is putting the information across in a different manner, you can feel "interested" and "stimulated" by these new thoughts. You may feel "energized" to find that someone has had the same problems that you are facing, and can suggest a solution to you. These emotions can be evoked in many different ways.

Why is this? We know the average experiences that customers have today are in general either poor or at best bland. Few Customer Experiences are good. It is disappointing that the same applies in the social media context, but unfortunately it is not surprising. This is a reflection of the organization that creates this experience and how customer-centric it is. If it is product-focused instead of customer-focused, you can expect its social media experiences to reflect a product focus.

In his second book, *Revolutionize your Customer Experience*, Colin outlines that all organizations are on a journey from naïve to natural in the way they are oriented around the customer; in other words, how customer-centric they are varies greatly. An orientation is the mindset that an organization has towards the customer. Let us give you an example. If your boss asks you to work late, what do you reply? If you are family-oriented you might say, "No, I can't work late as I need to see my family." If you are career-oriented you would say, "Yes, that would be fine." So in the same set of circumstances you take different actions depending on your orientation. The same applies to an organization in the way it is oriented around the customer. The book explains that

100

there are four possible orientations of an organization: naïve, transactional, enlightened, and natural. For more information we suggest you visit our website or engage with us over social media.

Our research indicated that the majority of organizations are transactional. They treat dealings with customers as transactions, something to be processed; they do not consider the emotional and subconscious side of the Customer Experience. They have not peeled back the onion of what the customer really wants; they typically only deal at a superficial level. They are miles away in terms of understanding the psychology of their customers. A large driver of the experience is "How much will it cost?" and what can be done to reduce the costs.

What this means is that most organizations deal with social media experiences in a transactional manner. Thus, they are getting the same results in the Destroying cluster of emotions as they do in other channels. Effectively they are repeating the same mistakes with their social media experience as they make in other channels, because that is their orientation; their mindset is the same.

Another significant effect is how social media experiences are established within the organization. Again, way back in 2002 Colin wrote about how new channels are born in organizations. We are seeing the same apply to social media experiences. Colin reminds us:

When any new channel is created it normally starts as someone's "pet project." In this case it will be someone with a passion for social media. They can see the future but the rest of the organization cannot. This person promotes the need to be in this new channel, and eventually manages to convince someone to give them a little funding. The organization sees it as an experiment as they are not certain this social media thing will catch on! It can be that the people that make these decisions are of the older age group, and typically they don't use social media personally and do not see their massive potential.

So the experiment is launched. Typically the integration with other established channels – call centers, shops, account managers – is poor, as it has not been fully thought through. As social media start to grow scalability becomes a problem, and the lack of integration with other channels starts to cause problems. Customers use different channels at different times depending on what suits them, and they expect the left hand to know what the right hand is doing within the organization. As the volumes increase the lack of strategic planning now starts to show, and we see the cracks. The cracks become gaps which then become chasms. Rather than solving problems the new channel is causing problems.

At the same time, as the volumes grow and people start to see the potential of social media, their use becomes a political football. Who should own the channel? What part of the business should it reside in? People see this politically as a threat to their empire, or an opportunity to grow it further. Battles are fought, won, and lost, while the customer still suffers. The organization responds by allocating more money and resources to the channel.

Remember "United breaks guitars." These gaps and chasms now spread in an instant over the Web. Everyone knows about the problems. Finally, senior execs get involved, a proper strategy is put in place, and the problems are sorted out. This happens only after customers have become annoyed, and customer loyalty is affected. Often considerable money and effort have been spent on plugging the gaps. We normally get a call at this point to help the organization sort the mess out and get a decent strategy in place. More forward-thinking companies engage us at the beginning of setting the strategy – which I have to say is cheaper!

To help guide you, whether your organization is in the set-up phase or at the point where things have got out of hand, there are a few steps in setting the strategy that we advise you to take.

Key questions of a social experience strategy

It is important that the social media experience is an integrated part of any customer strategy, and therefore it needs to be built within that context. The key strategic questions that need to be addressed for any social media experience implementation are:

- What is the Customer Experience you are trying to deliver in social media?
- What are the emotions you are trying to evoke in social media?
- Is your Customer Experience deliberate in social media?
- What do your customers really want from social media?
- What drives most value for the organization in social media?

The social media experience has its own demands, expectations, and characteristics, as we will discuss in the next chapter, and therefore the answers to these questions need to be answered in that context. Ideally, as Barry Judge indicated at the beginning of this chapter with the introduction of Twelpforce, social media can be used as a Trojan horse for getting other parts of the business to change.

In the next chapter we will continue to look at the results of our Emotional Signature® for social media experiences.

7 What drives or destroys a social media experience

Lionel Menchaca is the Chief Blogger at Dell. http://en.community. dell.com/ Dell has seen the power of the social media experience and has been active in the area. Lionel tells the story of what has been happening at Dell:

There's no shortage of folks who have been saying that social media is the next big thing. Dell jumped into the social media space more than three years ago. In those days we didn't spend a lot of time thinking about the larger implications of what we were doing. Back then, it was all about connecting and responding to customers and just making social media work. After starting with a blog we moved on to IdeaStorm, a way of involving with our customers in innovation. We then moved into Twitter and Facebook. We built a flickr page (which recently passed 1 million views) and a Dell YouTube channel to facilitate the sharing of picture and video content that we produced for Direct2Dell.

Looking at our online success in all those places the fundamentals were clear. The Web was an ideal place for us to connect directly with customers. Social media brought that and something more – a way to listen, learn, and engage with customers, with a clear emphasis on the "engage" part of the equation. It allows us to further those direct connections with customers while also sharing what we are all about, making technology work, work better and harder for you.

Today, as more and more customers are embracing social media, our thinking about Dell and the community has evolved beyond simply driving customers to our own sites. If you look at our aggregate presence on social media networks plus our own community sites, our worldwide community has grown to *more than 3.5 million people* across the social web. That's roughly a fan base the size of the population of Chicago. Our @DellOutlet is now close to 1.5 million followers on Twitter, and back in June we indicated that this had earned $3 million in revenue. Today it's not just Dell Outlet having success by connecting with customers on Twitter. In total, Dell's global reach on Twitter has resulted in more than *$6.5 million in revenue*. What does this mean to our customers and for Dell's social media strategy overall moving forward? In my mind, it boils down to a few key strategies for Dell:

■ Streamline our presence in social media networks, create meaningful content for customers, and continue to increase our connections with them in those places.

■ Focus on building a tighter integration between Dell.com, Support. Dell.com, and our Dell Community sites with our presence in social networks.

■ Continue our focus on scaling support of social media initiatives into the Dell business units.

For Dell, or any company for that matter, isolated social media efforts won't lead to long-term success in this space. Our long-term success depends on how well we execute on the key strategy points.

This a good example of a company that is embracing the social media experience to innovate its Customer Experience, engage with its customers, and drive profit. A social media experience has the potential to wield tremendous power. As we can see from the revenue increases, Dell is starting to harness this.

A key aspect of any social experience is the "six degrees of separation" between people. This phrase describes the degree to which people are interconnected. In a famous experiment in the 1960s, Stanley Milgram, a social psychologist in the United States, wanted to find out whether randomly selected people could get to know each other. In his experiment, he picked people from a few cities in the United States. The cities were chosen for geographic location and their social differences. He set these people a task, to get a package to a stockbroker in Boston, Massachusetts. The catch was that they could only do this through people they were on first-name terms with. So for example, if they didn't know the stockbroker but had a friend who lived near Boston, they could send the package to their friend because the friend might know the stockbroker, or someone else who knew the stockbroker. The experiment showed that on average it took six people to get to the stockbroker, hence "six degrees of separation."

When you consider that people now have their contacts on various social media sites, this is where six degrees of separation really comes to life. You can literally see who is connected to whom. LinkedIn, as an example, shows you how far you are away from a person you might wish to talk to. It also indicates whom you need to talk to in order to reach them. Understanding people networks is like gold dust from a commercial perspective. A number of organizations are undertaking research today to try to identify patterns to see how we are connected with each other. From a marketing perspective, this could be of enormous benefit. A great example of early attempts to harness this power is Dell Swarm.

This is based on the principle of harnessing your network to form a group of people to "group buy" PCs at a reduced price. This is how it works: you decide you want a new PC. Dell guarantees to sell its PCs for the lowest price on the Web to people in the swarm. As you wish to get the price of your PC lower, you encourage more of your friends to take part. As the swarm gets larger, the price reduces further. This is a win/win for everyone. This is a great use of social media, and starts to realize the enormous power of connections.

Groupon is another example of harnessing the power of these networks (www.groupon.com). This website is based in local cities in the United States. The same principles apply as to the Dell Swarm. The more people who buy, a product the cheaper it is. Every day people who subscribe to Groupon (which is free of charge) are sent information on the latest "Groupon" offers. One example of an offer recently was for a company selling specialized food which would normally retail for $40.[1] Via Groupon it was selling at $15. These offers need to attract enough people to make it worthwhile for the company concerned, so a minimum target is set. As customers know this and are attracted by the price, it is in their interests to promote the deal to their friends and family. Promoting this via social media is the most efficient and obvious way. In this example 1,200 signed up for the deal!

Steve Sickel, Senior Vice President, IHG, provides another example:

> We floated a special incentive to stay at our hotels to 150 of our customers on our US private community, and we encouraged these customers to pass it along to anyone they thought would find value in it. In six weeks the promotion virally spread to thousands of people from over 30 countries who drove more than $300,000 of incremental revenue to our hotels. In fact, we had one community member who forwarded the promotion to over 1,300 others, and what's even more interesting is, she didn't even participate in the promotion. She was a frequent customer of ours who had recently left her job to be a stay-at-home mum, but she still had a lot of frequent traveler friends. That's the power of social marketing.

In each of these cases we are seeing these companies use their customers' social networks to sell their products. Inevitably this will be a growing trend.

In addition and most importantly, we are seeing these organizations "engage" with their customers, which is essential to gain the maximum

---

1 http://abclocal.go.com/ktrk/story?section=news/consumer&id=7083827

benefit from a social media experience. There are four aspects to the meaning of "engage" according to Dictionary.com, and we believe organizations should be aiming to achieve all of them within the social media context.

- To occupy the attention or efforts of (a person or persons): *He engaged her in conversation.*
- To attract and hold fast: *The novel engaged her attention and interest.*
- To attract or please: *His good nature engages everyone.*
- To bind, as by pledge, promise, contract, or oath; make liable: *He engaged himself to repay his debt within a month.*

The word "engage" starts to move us back to experience psychology. Let's take each of these descriptions and see how it applies to a social media experience.

- "To occupy the attention" reminds us of the "attention cluster" of emotions in the Emotional Signature®.
- "To attract and hold fast" reminds us of customer loyalty and customer retention.
- "To attract or please" reminds us of customer acquisition and "pleased" being in the Advocacy clusters of emotions.
- "To bind, pledge, etc." reminds us that one way of building trust is to do what we say we are going to do.

Therefore, this word "engagement" is a good bridge between the rational and emotional parts of the experience. Steve from IHG has a great way of explaining why engagement is so important.

> I equate social media to a dinner party. It's an opportunity for me to engage with people who I know and an opportunity for me to meet new people who I don't know. It's an opportunity for me to share stories and information and gather new information and insights.
>
> Rather than throwing a huge party where we just invite the world, we started our parties with people who we already knew. This helped us start to change the mindset at IHG. Giving customers a seat at the table, having them be part of the dialogue, having them be part of the creation process, is the way we wanted to move forward to engage with customers and not just IHG broadcasting one-way messages.
>
> I could try to be the centre of all the conversation at my dinner party, and with four people I could probably manage that. But as the party gets to 8, 10, 12, 20 people, there's no way I can be the centerpiece of the conversation. I need other people to carry the conversation for me. That's what

we're finding in our public community. We encourage customers to answer business questions for other customers. This is far more powerful than us answering the questions.

So now by opening up a lot more widely and giving our advocates an opportunity to speak, it suddenly becomes a really active party with hundreds of people made up of dozens of conversations between three and four people.

To try and tap into this reservoir of information, insight, and ideas, we've started conversations on all different kinds of topics. We have asked customers' advice on our marketing approach. We've asked advice on campaigns we're considering. We've asked advice on the in-hotel experience. And the suggestions we get back go a long way to improving our overall Customer Experience.

This demonstrates the power of engaging with customers. Let's take Steve's analogy of a party one stage further as a lead into the rest of the results of the Emotional Signature® research.

Now imagine you are at a house party. Imagine you have just arrived and you don't know anyone. You are greeted at the door and walk into the main room. You walk over to a group who are standing around in a small circle, and someone is talking. No one says hello. You listen while one person is talking. He talks and talks and then talks some more. Occasionally one of the people in the circle tries to make a point, but the speaker is in broadcast mode and ignores them. You can't get a word in edgeways.

As you feel ignored and neglected, you leave that circle of people and join a second group. You notice this is a far more interactive group. As you walk over, everyone acknowledges you in a friendly manner. You notice people are engaging with each other in two-way conversation. You struggle to identify who is the leader. You are encouraged to take part, as one person says, "Tell us what you think." Others acknowledge your point of view. "That's a good point," and "That's interesting," they say. You enter more and more into the conversation; it's like chatting with old friends. It's informal, no one is trying to hog the conversation, and everyone is engaging. Before you know it two hours have passed and you wonder where the time has gone. What a nice group of people. you think. I would like to meet them again!

Which group do you prefer, group one or group two? It's obvious – group two. In group one the person was in broadcast mode and couldn't care less about you. They were not interested in you; they were only interested in themselves. No one welcomed you or encouraged you to speak. The leader was obvious and everyone was subservient to him. Did you feel they respected your opinion? No, they didn't know what your opinion was, and sadly, you could have had a great insight to share. How did group one make you feel? Probably frustrated, neglected, and irritated. These are all emotions that destroy value.

As we outlined in the maturity model in the last chapter, this is what most companies do when they entering into social media. They are in broadcast mode, not engaging mode. They are treating people like they treat them in the real world, but the rules are different in a social media experience.

Group two is the exact opposite. The group was engaging, and there wasn't an obvious leader. Everyone was encouraged to take part and respected your opinion. As people referred to your comments this made you feel important, and this engaging experience increased your self-esteem. In short, you felt accepted.

Here is the surprise – although it's not really a surprise. Getting back to our research with www.Customerthink.com and the Emotional Signature we spoke about in the last chapter, guess what the top five attributes were for an experience that drives value for an organization? Can't guess? Well, if you want to build a social media experience that drives value for your organization, our research shows the following are the five top attributes an organization needs to focus on, in order of priority:

1   The level of encouragement I receive to post my comments and express my opinion.
2   The respect I get from others.
3   The feeling I am important.
4   The sense of self-esteem I get.
5   The feeling that I am accepted.

Table 7.1 Comparing parties and social media experiences

Attending a party	Social media experience equivalent
You receive an invitation	You receive a request to join from a friend
You turn up at the door	You go onto the site for the first time
You are welcomed by the host	There are instructions about how you should join
You are shown where everything is	You take a look around and navigate the site easily
You mingle with the attendees	You post your comments and views
You move from group to group	You post your comments and views
You decide to leave	You log off
You thank your host and say goodbyes	You log off and get a message – Hey don't be away long! Or something like this.
You talk about the party	You read what other people have written about your comments

Please note, this is not about the number of pictures on a web page, the speed of the page, or how pretty it looks. These are important, but not as important as these fundamental human needs. We find it amazing that all too many organizations have lost sight of that. This is the secret sauce!

Just look at Table 7.1, which shows how the party experience and the social media experience are similar.

Again let's spend a bit more time delving down into this and going into more detail, with our experience psychology hat on and using the Emotional Signature® research. We have the attributes of the social media experience that we discussed in the last chapter. Effectively what we are trying to do is to distribute them across the grid shown in Figure 7.1. The vertical axis is whether the attribute of the experience drives value or not. Remember value could be revenue, customer retention, customer loyalty, brand, net promoter, or any other measure

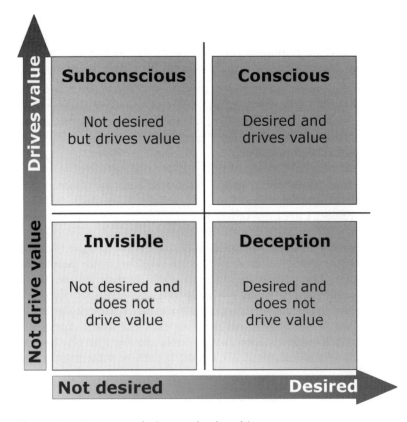

Figure 7.1 Customer desires and value drivers

you wish to define. The horizontal axis looks at whether the customer desires something or not. Therefore the boxes are as follows:

Conscious – Desired and drives value. The "desired" aspects of this research show the things customers know they want. They can tell you they want these, hence they are conscious. On the other axis we can statistically prove whether the desire drives or destroys value.

Subconscious – These are the things that customers don't say they want or desire. In other words they are not in the conscious mind. However we can prove they have a statistical link to value – hence they are subconscious. The subconscious experience is something we have explained in previous chapters.

Deception – This is the really interesting area. These are the things that customers say they desire, but that do not drive value. Therefore, you have to manage customer expectations with these if you determine that you are not going to provide them.

Invisible – These do not drive value nor are they desired by customers. Ask yourself, "Why are we doing them?" It could be that some of the attributes here are regulatory, or things the organization needs to undertake as part of its process. Ideally you wouldn't do these.

As we segmented the Emotional Signature® research into three segments of personal, business, and customer social media experience, it is interesting that the following two attributes appear in "conscious" for the customer social experience but "subconscious" in the personal and business social experience.

- the level of encouragement I receive to post my comments and express my opinion
- the respect I get from others.

We would suggest this is because, as customers, we are used to being asked for our opinion and encouraged to take part, since people want our custom. Also people know that you should treat customers with respect (which is not to say it always happens). Therefore, these are "conscious" in the customer social media experience environment but "subconscious" in the personal and business social media experiences.

To understand each context it is important we drill down to the next level of understanding. We'll look at each of these in turn. As a reminder:

A **personal social media experience** involves someone who uses social media in their personal life to interact with customers.

A **business social media experience** involves using social media in the business context: for example, cruising blogs on LinkedIn to do with business.

A **customer social media experience** involves using social media as a customer – investigating a holiday on TripAdvisor, on a blog doing research, or researching what TV to buy, for instance.

Finally, it is worth saying that this research is generic across all businesses. We get a different set of results for each different industry sector and for each company within the sector. These are treated as top-level guidance. To understand what drives value for your organization specifically, we would need to undertake an Emotional Signature® of the organization.

The Emotional Signature® for personal social media experiences

It is worth mentioning that social media experiences on Facebook and other social media have been predominantly amongst the younger age groups. However, this is now starting to change. The 35–54 demographic is starting to grow very quickly, with a rise of 276 percent in 2008–09. The 55+ group has grown by 194 percent.[2] Therefore, while the younger crowd are still the most frequent users, the older age group are quickly catching up, as they see the benefits and want to stay connected to their children via these media.

Our research shows those with personal social media experiences are significantly more positive about their experience than business and customer users. You can see in the emotional profile (see Figure 7.2) that we have measured the emotional engagement of personal social media experiences against the "overall social media" results. We have also measured this against the overall business index. You will recall that this business index is from our original research with London Business School, and accounts for all channels, all experiences, across all markets – theoretically an average Customer Experience.

Finally, you will also see from the stars in the figure that most of the emotions show a statistically significant difference between personal social media experiences and the overall social media results. Later you will see this is not the case for business and customer media social experiences. The only emotions that are not significantly different

---

2 http://www.istrategylabs.com/2009/01/2009-facebook-demographics-and-statistics-report-276-growth-in-35-54-year-old-users/

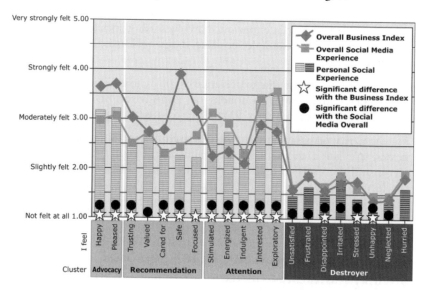

Figure 7.2 Emotional profile: personal social media experience

in the personal social media experience context are "focused" and "hurried."

Bearing in mind that the lower the bars are on the Destroyer cluster, the better the result is, as this means these emotions are not being felt. We can see that the results of the Destroyer cluster of emotions are better in the personal social media experience than for "overall social media," and are about on par with the overall business index, the average Customer Experience. Why is this the case? In our view, sites like Facebook and MySpace have been built primarily with personal social media experiences in mind. Over time these platforms have refined their offerings to meet the personal social media experience requirements. Now as people see this success, they have started to invent business and customer applications. These have been shoehorned into what is largely a personal social media experience environment. However it must be recognized that some platforms are purpose built for business; LinkedIn is a good example.

Two specific attributes in the personal social media experience that need to be improved are:

■ Trustworthiness of the information. Organizations are not doing a good job in these areas for the personal social media experience. As we all know, the trustworthiness of the information is about the people who put information on the system, and therefore it unfortunately reflects the people who place information there – people's friends and family.

■ Security of the media. Security is a natural worry. We have all heard stories of accounts being hacked, and with so much personal information on these sites, providers must focus on this.

It is worthy of note that the vast majority of attributes for personal social media experiences are in the subconscious arena and do not get picked up in normal research. Here are the main attributes that need to be addressed when building a personal social media experience that drives value:

Subconscious

This accounts for 69 percent of the total attributes in a personal social media experience. Top attributes to focus on are:

■ The opportunities that allow me to express myself. The great thing about social media is that you can do what you wish and follow any pursuit you choose. We saw an example of this with Tammy's recipes and her tea bag cover collecting. In your tribe you feel you are able to be yourself. You can express your true self, you don't have to put on a pretence for work.

■ The opportunity to become creative. Again in your tribe you can experiment in a safe environment.

Conscious

This accounts for 15 percent of the total attributes in a personal social media experience.
Top attributes to focus on are:

■ The use of pictures. There is nothing better than looking at photos of the party you have just attended or the holiday you have been on with your friends. Clearly, this is a demonstration of belonging to a group. Showing personal pictures is a demonstration that you trust your "tribe" and that you are willing to share. There are pictures that you would not show to just anyone. Also the famous comment, "A picture is worth a thousand words," is very relevant here.

■ The extent to which the content is entertaining. In the personal social media experience one of the key reasons people are interacting is for entertainment. Therefore they are looking for some entertaining content.

■ The ability to make new friends/contacts. Through the six degrees of separation you can start to extend your contacts and feel more connected with other people's lives, extending your tribe and the feeling of belonging.

To be very clear, we are not saying emotional aspects of the Customer Experience are the only answer. There are clearly physical and rational items that also play a part in a good social media experience. In fact the physical and rational aspects of any experience can drive emotions.

Let us now look at the business social media experience.

The Emotional Signature® for business social media experiences

Barry Judge, Chief Marketing Officer of Best Buy, says:

> When I am using social media in business I'm hearing things that I never would hear in my "real" life. There is something about this virtual environment that makes conversations more open, less restricted by title, function, and whatever barriers, real or imagined, people bring to what they do.
>
> It's easier to connect with the outside world. I can't put my finger on why access happens more freely, except to say I feel bonded in a way with others who are jumping into this pool with me and are trying to figure this new wave out. I also like to think of myself as a very curious person, and Twitter is turning me on to cool things. I feel there is no better way for me personally to reinforce being transparent and honest across the organization than by showing these behaviors by participating in activities like Twitter and blogging. My goal is to be more easily accessible for the entire company, not just the people that I directly work with. This medium gives me that opportunity, and everyone else the ability to participate if they so choose.

There are a number of advantages of a social media experience in the business to business environment. We can see in Figure 7.3 the emotional profile of the business social media experience. None of the emotions that drive or destroy value are significantly different from the overall social media experience.

When comparing the business social media experience against the overall business index (the average Customer Experience), we see that some emotions are worse, some better. We have outlined them in Table 7.2.

In looking at the emotions that are significantly better, you note that with the expectation of "disappointment" these are in the Attention cluster of emotions. People still find this information novel. They are

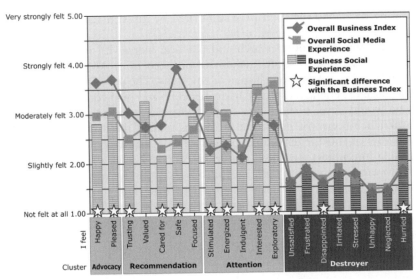

Figure 7.3 Emotional profile: business social media experience

"stimulated" by these media; they want to "explore" their use; they are "energized" and get a buzz from the activity; it piques their "interest." Barry Judge has an example of how these emotions can manifest themselves in the business social media experience.

> I recently tweeted about the book I was reading, *What would Google Do?* and said I really liked it. The next morning I got a tweet back from Jeff Jarvis who wrote the book, saying, "Hey, thanks for the tweet on the book." I contacted him back and asked if he was interested in coming in and talking to us about the book, and how it might apply to Best Buy. He agreed, so that's what we did. It took a minimal amount of time, and without social media this would have been far more difficult to arrange and been far too formal.

Table 7.2 Comparing the business social media experience and the overall business index

Significantly better	Significantly worse
Stimulated	Happy
Energized	Pleased_
Interested	Trusting
Exploring	Cared for
Disappointed	Safe
	Hurried

Clearly Barry and the team were stimulated by this contact and gained a lot out of it.

We know from our research and practical work with many clients in this arena that to retain customers you need to evoke the Recommendation and Attention clusters of emotions. The use of social media for social experiences can have many benefits, and help connect people who would never normally have met. With the business social media experience the most important attributes remain the same as above: the level of encouragement people get; feeling that they are respected; feeling important; the sense of acceptance, and a sense of self-esteem. However if you wish to drive customer satisfaction specifically and the levels of trust in the business environment, you need to focus on the following attributes as well. Again we have split these into conscious and subconscious.

Conscious

These account for 20 percent of the total attributes in a business social media experience. The top attributes to focus on are:

- The creative ideas I come across.
  The business social media experience is where people try to find information to help them, and ideally these ideas will not just be a regurgitation of old ideas. Creative ideas, new thoughts, are what is important.
- The helpfulness of the links.
  Again, this applies to people looking for new information. The Web is a big place, so finding useful information is key.
- The quality of the information I come across.
  Quality, not quantity is key.

Subconscious

These account for 60 percent of the attributes in a business social media experience. The top attributes to focus on are:

- The extent to which the content is entertaining.
  This shows the value of looking at the subconscious side of the experience. Not many people in the business environment would say they want information to be entertaining, but in reality that's what they would prefer. Colin does a lot of conference speaking, and he makes his speeches humorous so people enjoy the performance, but he also get over the important business messages.

■ The level to which new information makes me think differently.
Building on the creative ideas, people want to think differently.
This is probably why you are reading this book. You want to see
things from a different perspective.

■ The novelty of the information I come across.
A subset of entertaining and creative, it needs to be new, fresh, and
original.

If you looked at all of these attributes together they could be seen as
the way to evoke the desired emotions. Let us explain further. What
emotions do you feel when you come across creative ideas? You might
feel energized: you want to explore this idea, and are stimulated and
interested. The same applies with the "new information that makes you
think differently." Thus these attributes evoke the Attention cluster of
emotions.

It is interesting to note that in a business social media experience
there is a need to be entertaining and a need to consider novel ways of
getting the information across. Business can be very boring and dry.
To energize people, to make it stimulating and interesting, information
needs to be spiced up and not delivered in the same old boring way.

Another aspect of the business use of social media is in customer
research. A number of organizations are now using tools to dip into
streams of data and see what customers are saying instead of using
the traditional methods of asking customers questions. In addition,
organizations are engaging with customers to gain feedback on their
Customer Experience, and then set in place improvement plans. Dell
Ideastorm is one such example. The following is taken from the
Dell website:

IdeaStorm was created to give a direct voice to our customers and an
avenue to have online "brainstorm" sessions to allow you the customer to
share ideas and collaborate with one another and Dell. Our goal through
IdeaStorm is to hear what new products or services you'd like to see Dell
develop. We hope this site fosters a candid and robust conversation about
your ideas.

In almost three years, IdeaStorm has crossed the 10,000 idea mark and
implemented nearly 400 ideas! As Dell is always moving forwards and
innovating, so is IdeaStorm. In addition to the open discussion IdeaStorm
site, in December 2009, Dell added "Storm Sessions" where Dell posts a
specific topic and asks customers to submit ideas. These Storm sessions will
only be open for a limited time, therefore makes Storm Session discussions
targeted, relevant and time-bound.

Through IdeaStorm and Storm Sessions, our commitment is to listen to
your input and ideas to improve our products and services, and the way we

do business. We will do our best to keep you posted on how Dell brings customer ideas to life. Welcome and enjoy IdeaStorm![3]

Before we leave the business social media experience, let's take a few minutes to look at the whole area of trust. As you will be aware this is becoming very important to business. You can see from the emotional profile that the levels of trust in the business social media experience are higher than the "overall social media" but not as high as the "business index" (average Customer Experience). Whole books have been written on this subject, so we don't intend to go into any detail here, other than to say that trust comes through transparency. As we have heard, a social media experience is built on this. Do not try to hoodwink people. This is the wrong medium for that to happen.

Barry Judge has another good example of transparency in the social media experience.

I am interested in the concept of transparency. I got involved in Twitter and blogging and found that by being open and talking about the challenges and opportunities in my job I could connect with a pretty bright group of people externally and, importantly, people within a company, people that work in marketing, people that work in other parts of the corporation, people that work in the field. The more I could open up my thinking the more people would have context for it, they would know what I'm working and thinking about, and have the ability to impact what I was thinking. As I got into it I also found I could be an example for others. Not many people at my level were interacting with social media, and I believe this is important in building trust across the organization.

We would suggest that most organizations would like to become the "trusted advisor" of their customers. As a trusted advisor you would be even-handed and advise customers based on longer-term knowledge. This will pay you dividends.

In the business and customer environment we are starting to see the rise of another kind of trusted advisor, or what we would call an "authority." Let us explain.

When buying a car or house insurance on the Web, how do you compare company prices? A few years ago you would have needed to visit each company website to obtain a quote (see Figure 7.4). Today you only have to go to an "aggregator" site to undertake the same task (see Figure 7.5). These sites are now quite common. In the United Kingdom, Confused.com is an example, and in the United States a good example is www.insureme.com. On an aggregator site you input your

---

3 http://www.ideastorm.com/ideaAbout?pt=About+IdeaStorm

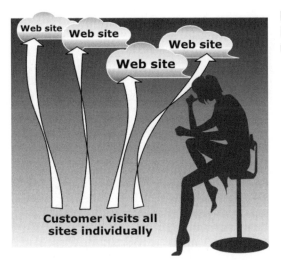

Figure 7.4
How we used to research the Web

Figure 7.5
How we research the Web today

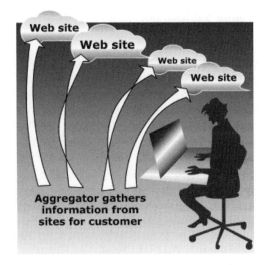

data once, then the site gathers the information from each company and presents a comparison. This obviously saves time for customers. It's an advantageous solution for the customer and the aggregator, but it further drives commoditization in the insurance market, which disintermediates offerings at this critical point of decision making.

What does this have to do with a social media experience, you might ask? The same is happening with information in social media for business social experiences. The challenge from a social experience perspective is the number of different blogs and platforms that are out there today. How do you read all the blogs and keep up to date?

Figure 7.6 How the authority works

To overcome this we are starting to see the aggregation of social media information. For example LinkedIn, Facebook and Twitter now have an "interested status" update. Update one and they are all updated. Everyone wants to be the "main" social media site, and this war is only at the beginning. Consolidation is the natural way of things. One thing is for certain, the landscape will not look the same in five years' time.

The same principle applies to blogs. Let us explain. Colin subscribes to Google reader, and links to between 20 and 30 sites using RSS. He gets constant feeds from these sites. The good news is that being with Google Reader means he doesn't have to visit these sites individually, as Google Reader does that for him. The bad news is that there are still far too many articles to read, and with the explosion of social media and many organizations now realizing they need to play in this space, the problem is set to become worse before it becomes better. The issue is, how do you sort the good information from the bad?

As usual, it's the 80/20 rule. Only 20 percent of the articles are worth reading. The challenge is in sifting through the 80 percent to find the 20 percent of gems. Enter the aggregators, or authorities, of information. A good example of this is http://mashable.com/, "The social media guide." It gathers information from many different sources, and provides a good overview of social media. It is an "authority." An authority is a person or organization who is seen as an expert in their subject, someone who has proven themselves to be a trusted source of information and is respected. They know what they are talking about and they have a track record in the subject.

An authority can weld great power as they become the funneling point of information. Herein lies the danger. If you are not an authority you are an also-ran. Like the insurance companies, the danger is that your site will be disintermediated from your audience.

That brings us to a close on the business social media experience. Let's turn our attention to the final part of the research.

The Emotional Signature® for customer social media experiences

Elisa Haidt is Senior Marketing Manager overseeing student marketing at Adobe. She shares with us a successful social media campaign she conducted for students, called Real or Fake.

> Real or Fake was a really engaging experience we provided for our student customers on Facebook. We wanted to make it really fun and for them to see the value of Adobe products, to understand why they might want to buy our products, and to show them the discounts we could provide.
>
> Real or Fake was developed to support the launch of the Adobe Student Editions [Adobe products sold at a discount for students] in North America. The concept of the game was simple: could people tell the difference between a real or fake photo? The "fake" photos had been manipulated by Adobe products, and a tutorial popped up which showed the users what they could do with our software.
>
> It ran for four weeks and we had great results. Just in week one we had over 53,000 page views. Before the campaign ran we had 11,500 fans on Facebook, and today we have over 40,000.
>
> This was really the beginning of a push to increase our community and engage with students. This was about engaging with them where they already are. The game was played 5,459 times in that first week by over 3,300 unique users. 40 percent played the game again, and we had 22 percent of those who then clicked further on a link that said "See how we did it." When you click on this link there was a very brief tutorial which started by saying, "If you had this image and you had Adobe Photoshop, this is how you would do it."
>
> We had a lot of engagement and students learned about how they could do something like that. The biggest metrics for us at this time were that 6 percent of those who played clicked on "share the link," and 6 percent clicked on "buy now," in that first week! It was a great success.

This is a good example of how you can succeed in a customer social media experience.

As we can see from the emotional profile in the customer social media experience, the only significant difference between the customer social media experience and the overall social media is "indulgent." At the moment many customers do not think of social media as a normal way to shop, and consider it a bit of a luxury.

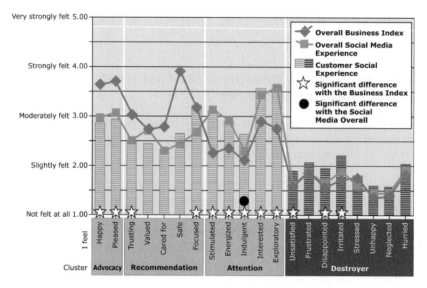

Figure 7.7 Emotional profile: customer social media experience

Again if we look at which emotions score significantly better or worse than the overall business index, they are as shown in Table 7.3.

Once more we see the Attention cluster of emotions coming to the fore. In addition, there are more from the significant Destroyer cluster of emotions in the customer social media experience than in personal and business.

Customers compare their social media experience with a normal customer experience, and find it wanting.

As customers we expect the same type of interaction with a company as we would get in the real world. However, the company's stage of maturity (look back to Figure 5.2) can impact on this.

Table 7.3 Comparing the customer social media experience and the overall business index

Significantly better	Significantly worse
Focused	Happy
Stimulated	Pleased
Energised	Trusting
Indulgent	Dissatisfied
Interested	Disappaointed
Exploring	Irritated

Colin provides an example of a disappointing social media experience:

> I was speaking at a conference in Denver and staying at the Renaissance Hotel. I was very surprised to find the hotel charged $12.95 for internet access and $5 for a bottle of water in my room. I decided to take pictures of the signs and post the image to Twitter with comments. As I had been talking to a few hotel groups about their social media strategy, I was also interested to see what the response from Renaissance would be. I was disappointed, as I heard nothing. In fact, the only thing that happened was that the next day the company started to follow me on Twitter! I had thought it was going to follow me to allow us to connect over Twitter and then it would address my comments. I hadn't expected a refund; I had just expected some form of acknowledgement. But nothing happened. I was disappointed.

What do you need to do to start providing a great customer social media experience and drive value? Again let's repeat this from above, as these are the main attributes to focus on in priority order, but note that some have moved from conscious to subconscious attributes:

Conscious

1   The level of encouragement I receive to post my comments and express my opinion.
2   The respect I get from others.

Subconscious

3   The feeling I am important.
4   The sense of self-esteem I get.
5   The feeling that I am accepted.

All of these are basic human needs. It is therefore essential that you "engage" with customers, and treat them as if they are coming to a party and you are the best host in the world!

If we ask you to cast your mind back a moment, you will recall from the previous chapter that we used different value indicators to measure the experiences. You can then highlight different attributes to focus on. Therefore, if you wish to improve your net promoter score or customer loyalty in the customer social media experience, you will need to address these attributes as well:

Conscious

This accounts for 20 percent of the total attributes in a customer social media experience. The top attributes to focus on to improve customer loyalty and net promoter are:

1   The speed of finding relevant information. A typical physical/ rational attribute. This is about not just the speed of the line, but how quickly people get to the right information the number of clicks.
2   The helpfulness of the links posted by others. With the massive amount of data on the Web, finding the right information is key.

Subconscious

This accounts for 20 percent of the total attributes in a customer social media experience. The top attributes to focus on to improve customer loyalty and net promoter are:

3   The ease of use of social media. Ease of use is a key aspect of any Customer Experience.
4   The speed of access over the internet. It is important that your sites do not slow the access down.
5   The opportunities that allow me to express myself. Again we are seeing the human part of the customer coming out here. Expressing one's self as an individual is key.
6   The informal writing style. A social media experience and formality don't mix! A more informal style is more effective.

Finally, another significant value indicator we looked at that in this environment is the trustworthiness of the experience. A survey by Nielson showed that 90 percent of consumers online trusted what their friends and family told them and 70 percent trusted what other customers had written online.[4] Our Emotional Signature® research shows there are a number of attributes that are destroying trustworthiness:

■   The novelty of the information I come across. If the information is novel for the sake of being novel it can drive a lack of trust.
■   The ability to send a direct message. If someone cannot send a direct message, this drives a lack of trust. Why can't you communicate with the sender? Social media is meant to be about a conversation.
■   The ease of receiving direct messages. The same again. We have all written to people over social media and not received replies.
■   The speed of getting replies. If you don't reply for a number of days, people will assume that you have ignored them, and again this drives down trust. It really annoys us when you email a company and the reply is that it will get back to you in five days. 24 hours

---

4   http://blog.nielsen.com/nielsenwire/consumer/global-advertising-consumers-trust-real-friends-and-virtual-strangers-the-most/

maybe, but five days is ridiculous, and shows they are not really serious. This is email, social media are even more demanding.

It is also interesting to note that "novelty of information" was a positive attribute in the business social media experience environment but is a negative in the customer environment. Therefore the message is that customer segmentation is important!

There is a great deal to think about in the customer social media experience, because customers already have expectations of the brands they deal with, and expect an acceptable level of service. I think we have demonstrated the power of this, if you can get it right. If this interaction with customers works well, the results can be great. Laree Daniel, Senior Vice President at Aflac, comments:

> While Aflac's venture into the world of social media remains in its infancy, we have already experienced overwhelmingly positive results. We've been very pleased to see the Aflac duck on Facebook exceed 160,000 fans in six months and about 3,300 followers on Twitter, numbers that are steadily growing on a daily basis. The duck's recent Facebook campaign also generated $1.16 million for the Aflac Cancer Center and 851,215 new members for the Aflac Cancer Center Cause.
>
> We are in the process of defining an end-to-end measurement model that is aligned with enterprise business objectives and are confident that the ROI on Social will be significant.
>
> On a more strategic level, we've been able to help our Field Force and customers better understand why we do what we do, and utilize their feedback to examine our own processes and decisions.

Finally a big change that is taking place as we write this book is "real time" search: in other words, seeing what people are writing in that moment. This means that when you search for a company using Google, not only will Google provide you with a list of the websites you can visit, it will show you the real-time conversations that are happening at that moment. Now imagine that you are searching for a company and you see real-time feeds that are talking about a poor experience people have had with that company. Do you think this will influence your decision of which one to look at? Of course it will. This will be a major factor in organizations wanting to engage over social media and address customer issues.

To summarize the last three chapters, moving forward, social media and a personal social media experience are going to be a massive part of a new Customer Experience. Any organization that is putting its head in the sand in the hope these media will go away is naive. We would encourage you to embrace this change and use the research we have undertaken to point you in the right direction. We'll leave the final words to Barry Judge, Chief Marketing Officer from Best Buy:

> Where do I think social media is going? I think everything's going to be open so you might as well figure out how to be open yourself now. Information is going to be very available everywhere, all of it, and I think that "social shopping" is coming somehow, that is, communities of people that want to buy things together. Finally I think that there are going to be businesses that are built off social media conversations. In short it will be everywhere.

As we leave the subject of a social experience we now turn our attentions to the more distant future, and show you some of the other work we are involved with in looking to the future. Understanding a person's brain is the focus of the science known as neuroscience. While a great deal about the brain is still not known, we can see the day when we will be able to tap into customers' thoughts and not ask them questions. Let us explain further in the next few chapters.

8 The brain's experience – opening the black box

The concept of neuroexperience

In the opening scene in the 2002 movie *Minority Report*, John Anderton (played by Tom Cruise) walks through a shopping mall. The year was supposedly 2038. In that scene, John Anderton's eyes are scanned and the interactive billboards are instantly changed or customized to fit John Anderton's likes and preferences. The ads call out to John Anderton as he walks by. This is the most straightforward future that can be predicted by the melding of neuroscience to business. It does not require a large leap of foresight (though perhaps it required a bit more in 2002). It is straightforward because it simply shows what might happen to advertising as it progresses towards one-to-one marketing. Believe it or not, the practical application of this has already started to be tested and deployed on our very real streets. We will speak about this in more detail a little later.

> This is just the beginning of *the* future world of what we call "neuroexperience."

The idea that we can know what is actually happening in a Customer Experience at the really detailed level (anatomically, and eventually at the molecular level) is attractive and desirable for a number of reasons. Achieving this is the burgeoning space of neuroexperience – the exploration and development of techniques and applications from the world of neuroscience applied to Customer Experience. With this we could develop much more accurate customer metrics and predictive models. If we had a clearer understanding of the mechanisms underlying how we actually think and feel, we could better study and understand how customers will behave. When we say "actually feeling," we need this literally. For example, we might be able to say that a specific customer is feeling trust at a specific point in the Customer Experience. The interesting bit is that the customer might

127

not know they are feeling trust, as this is only going on in their subconscious experience, and therefore if they were asked a question about how they were feeling, they would not be able to articulate it. The big difference between where we are today and where we will be is:

> Today we ask customers' opinion about how they feel. Tomorrow we will *see* how they feel.

When business is armed with this knowledge, it can affect the behaviors of consumers more effectively. Part of that understanding will explain underlying mechanisms that are subconscious to the consumer (such as emotions and moods), as we discussed in Chapter 2. Therefore our definition of a neuroexperience is:

> Neuroexperience is the experience the customer has at the neuro-anatomical, neuro-physical, neuro-chemical, and neuro-physiological levels. This experience often occurs subconsciously and is the result of interaction(s) between an organization and a customer.

The neuroexperience of course translates into customer behavior at some point.

In other words, the actual brain activity is subconscious. Keep in mind that all of your bodily functions are controlled by your brain. You are not aware of that brain activity, only its outcome – your heart beats, your hand moves, and so on. Likewise, in complex behaviors of the type we are generally concerned with in Customer Experience, there is much brain activity that goes on before the behavior is displayed.

It is this crossover from thought to action/behavior that businesses are interested in. Illuminating the neuroexperience is valuable because it will allow us to understand what a customer is really thinking, even when the customer may not be able to articulate it or predict behavior based on neuroexperience precursors.

That is to say, the exploration of customers' neuroexperience will give organizations a truth serum technology. Regardless of what customers may say or not say, neural methods are being developed which will allow businesses to know the neural source code behind customer attitudes and behaviors.

Just consider the value of understanding the neuroexperience (that is, being able to understand how customers really think or will behave) in the following circumstances:

- Although customer satisfaction scores remain high, a business notices steady customer attrition. Are the customers really satisfied or just saying so? If they are satisfied, what else is going on that is driving the attrition?

- What if it were determined that customers' neuroexperience "happiness" score was 30 percent below that of their expressed satisfaction on surveys?

■ A contact center gets lots of complaints about its service although all agents have received extensive training and net promoter score is relatively high. Wouldn't it be really useful to know exactly at which point in calls the operatives start to lose their customers?

- What if it were determined that customers' neuroexperience deteriorates whenever the word "probably" is mentioned?

The whole area of "neuro" is being looked at by many disciplines. You will increasingly find "neuro" being used as a prefix to many concepts – neuromarketing, neuroeconomics, neuroaccounting, and so on. Neuroeconomics has the longest and most established history. Neuroeconomics is the study of the brain's role in how we make decisions. Believe it or not, the first conference on neuroeconomics was held only in 2002, so it's that new. Another related field is neuromarketing – the applied study of how the brain responds to marketing stimuli. So as you can see a lot of activity is happening around the world, but not a lot of people know about this, as it is still a specialized subject and it can be complex.

Neuroexperience is a broader subject than neuromarketing, just as the discipline of Customer Experience is different from marketing. Clearly there are links between the two. When a customer experiences a brand this is often done via some sort of marketing. When they receive a direct mail from a marketing campaign this is part of their experience. Obviously, marketing plays a large role in Customer Experience. Neuroexperience refers to the effects an organization's marketing activity has on the brain.

Neuroexperience is therefore at a higher level, and includes the overall service interaction (operations, marketing, finance, and so on). One of the key things we have learned in Customer Experience is that the experience is not just determined by marketing activities. It includes word of mouth, customer service, and day-to-day operations. So how does the brain react to these experience? What can we learn from it? What drives most value?

Now let's explore *Minority Report*'s John Anderton's mall experience again. John was biometrically scanned for identification purposes. Biometrics is measurement of bodily features and characteristics (such as fingerprints or voice patterns). You may have seen some of this in some PCs today, in the form of fingerprint readers to use instead of passwords. The *Minority Report* scene shows an eye scan which allows

John to be identified accurately in real time as he walks down a corridor. This technology is in use today by some countries' passport and immigration services.

The United Kingdom for instance has a system called IRIS (iris recognition immigration system) which is based on an ocular (eye) scan of the iris portion of the eye (the colored ring around the pupil). IRIS identifies registered members because each us has a unique "iris-print." So identification based on an iris scan is secure and fraud-resistant. This makes it possible for a person to be identified simply by looking into a special camera.

The system requires people to be registered, where a snap shot of the iris is taken by a special high-definition camera. The resulting photo is digitized. When a registered British citizen walks through an IRIS channel at the airport, a quick photograph is taken and that photograph is compared with the iris snapshots in the database (see Figure 8.1). When a match is made the citizen is cleared for entry into the United Kingdom. The whole process at the airport takes about 20 seconds. IRIS registration takes about 10 minutes. Now imagine that

Figure 8.1 IRIS at work

everyone in the country has biometrics taken as the security levels increase, or even that people allow this information to be shared with companies to enable them to get discounts on goods.

This application is not as free-flowing as the John Anderton scene, but then the purpose is much more serious, and absolute accuracy is required. If the scanner was off in the John Anderton scene, the worst that could happen is that he might get ads meant for a close relative. An immigration service has no room for error – especially in these times.

Iris recognition is a form of biometrics that is a fast, secure, and fraud-resistant way to check a person's identity. Biometrics is the science of using digital technology to recognize a person from a physical characteristic (for example a fingerprint or iris pattern) or another unique personal characteristic (for example a voice pattern or handwriting).

While the *Minority Report* scene did not show the power of neuroexperience, it easily could have. What if the ads displayed were changed not just because John Anderton was identified accurately (using biometrics) but also because the system could identify his mood and intentions at that moment? This would be done through neuroexperience. The ads would be dependent not only on the fact that John Anderton was walking by, but on the knowledge that John Anderton was in a foul mood but wanted to buy a big-budget item right away! Maybe he was upset because he had been shopping for five hours already. Just by exploring the implications of this scenario, we can paint the neuroexperience picture outlined in Table 8.1. The advertising system is programmed to show different responses based on John and how he is feeling.

The choice of specific ad is pinpointed by what is going on inside customer. Even if, John Anderton were stopped by a field researcher and asked how he was feeling today, he might not and probably would not answer "I am feeling upset today," nor does John always telegraph his general buying mood to even experienced sales staff.

In effect, neuroexperience may be thought of as the burgeoning field of applied mind reading and cultivation. It will allow businesses to maximize value (over the short term, long term, and customer lifetime) by having a truer unbiased and unfiltered understanding of their customers, which will enable the business to:

■ meet, exceed (or even change) customers' expectations in subtle ways
■ effectively manage cost to serve and acquire.

What's the big deal?

For those readers who are not interested in vision and future paradigm shifts, the answer is that there is no big deal. Neuroexperience is at

Table 8.1 A neuroexperience example

Scenario	Mood	Shopping Intent	Advertisement
1	Good	Buying	Purchase-oriented ad
2	Foul	Looking	Mood-enhancing ad
3	Good	Looking	Product exposure ad
4	Foul	Buying	Purchase-oriented ad

an embryonic state as applied to business. The technology is being created as we speak, and our current knowledge of neuroexperience is rudimentary.

Where we are today with neuroexperience is akin to where we were in the 1960s with computers. Computers existed but they were not considered practical devices for the average business. Visionaries were beginning to realize how computers might change the nature of business to make it more efficient and productive. At the time, general knowledge of computers was in the hands of the few. Knowledge of higher-level programming languages was still rudimentary (by today's standards) and the technology was a bit bulky. Remember transistors had only begun to be used in popular electronics in the 1960s. Soon afterwards, the microchip was invented. Essentially, it was Bill Gates and Steven Jobs who figured out and capitalized on these advances for businesses of all shapes and sizes. The rest is the history that we continue to live. The point is that neuroexperience is about where computing was in the late 1960s, just before the sea change.

Three parameters are of central importance to neuroexperience:

- computational sophistication and power, size and portability of technology
- business vision
- acceptance.

To understand how the brain works and predict behavior, we need a massive amount of computing power to mimic the brain's activity. This is not really available today, but we all know of Moore's Law. In 1965, Gordon E. Moore stated that the number of transistors on a chip would double about every two years. This has come to be known as Moore's Law, and empirical evidence suggests that it is true. The impact of Moore's Law is that computing power, processing speed, and memory capacity are increasing geometrically. The difference is that the rate of computational power is advancing and size of technology is decreasing at close to exponential rates.

We also are seeing computational neuroscience develop and become more sophisticated at a rapid rate. Computational neuroscience is the study of the information-processing properties of brain functions and structures. Indeed, it was introduced as a field only in 1985. As was stated earlier, one of the criteria for neuroexperience is that it is non-invasive. Computational neuroscience is the approach that will allow this to happen.

The size of the technology is also of importance in neuroexperience, because it will need to be portable if it is to be used in the field, mimicking the application in *Minority Report*, or use massively fast transmissions if data is sent to central computers to be processed and sent back to the point of contact with the customer.

Computing power is one aspect of this miniaturization. Another is the development of nanotechnology – the science and technology of building devices, such as electronic circuits, from single atoms and molecules. In other words, in time we will be able to use equipment on the customer in the field rather than bringing the customer in to the lab, as is the current practice. Nanotechnology in fact offers even greater possibilities in the clinical realm. For example, it will be possible some day to inject the technology into the patient. This is not an ethical consideration for neuroscience

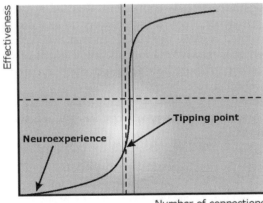

Figure 8.2 The tipping point for neuroexperience

because neuroexperience needs to be non-invasive. Likewise, it is unlikely that customers will want to be injected with "nanoneuroscanners." However, it is interesting to think about how such technology will evolve and eventually come to be used in neuroexperience. Already a camera has been developed that can fit inside a single brain cell, and take 1,000,000 frames per second. The resolution is not great yet, but it is in the early stages of production.

Business acceptance is happening more organically. Nevertheless, there is evidence of a tipping point (see Figure 8.2) on the horizon. We have started to see the first books on neuroexperience specifically written for a business audience. Additionally, the blogosphere and Twitterland are full of neuroexperience-related posts and links. Many of the oft-shared TED videos are focused on neuroscience. TED is a nonprofit conference bringing together people from three worlds: technology, entertainment, and design, devoted to ideas worth spreading. These TED videos are some of the most shared links in business-oriented social media.

We are on the cusp of technological/computational breakthroughs that will literally change the way we think of customers and business. Neuroexperience is in its infancy but it is beginning to emerge. It's as if the brain no longer wants to be in a black box – it is revealing itself to us. The choice managers have is to decide when they want to (not if they will) learn about neuroexperience, and its applications and opportunities.

Thomas J. Watson is often quoted as saying that "I think there is a world market for maybe five computers" in 1943. Although he was just about right in 1943, he was able to see further up that S curve. Bill Gates also looked up that curve in the early1970s.

If you are looking for business-ready applications that are not too far outside of current approaches, refer to the chapters on experience psychology. For the remaining readers, the big deal is that neuroexperience is a sea-change phenomenon. We are at the early stages of its formation, but visionaries will no doubt be able to spot the burgeoning opportunities that are becoming ripe for exploitation.

These will be highlighted in the following chapters. But before we explore the current and future states of neuroexperience, it is necessary that we cover a few brain basics.

Neuroscience for managers

It often seems that we've been trying to understand our brains for as long as we've had them. An organ capable of art, insight, of wisdom and wonder, ought to look the part – somehow spangly and luminous. Instead,

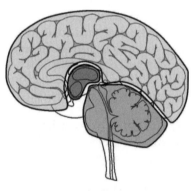

Figure 8.3 The human brain

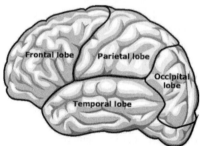

Figure 8.4 The four lobes of the brain

it's gray and lumpish. No wonder our efforts to fathom its workings have so frequently gone awry.

Jeffrey Kluger, *Your Brain: A User's Guide* (2009)

The difficulty is that the brain may look lumpish, and only weigh about 2.8 lb, representing only 2 percent of our bodyweight, but it is an immense universe of nerve cells. There are some 100 billion neurons packed into the brain. That number goes up to a whopping 1 trillion if we include all of the cells in the brain. Put in another way, the brain accounts for 20 percent of the human genome (of the 30,000 genes, 6,000 are expressed in the brain).

Brain real estate

The most valuable real estate in the world is inside your head – if only we had an accurate map. Essentially, that is the question. As you might imagine there has already been lots of work done to understand which parts of our brains are responsible for what thoughts and behaviors, and how they work. The fields of cognitive neuroscience and neuropsychology are all about answering this question. Cognitive neuroscience is concerned with how psychological and cognitive functions are produced by the brain. Neuropsychology is concerned the structure and function of the brain related to specific psychological processes and overt behaviors.

For our purposes, we need to understand that the brain is one of the last great frontiers. Just like pioneers learned to prospect for gold in the Wild West of the mid-1800s in the United States, neuroscientists are learning how to prospect in the brain. Even without the advanced techniques that are being utilized today, a great deal has already been learned about our valuable neural real estate.

We are going to give you a introduction to your brain. We will not go into any detail, but it is important to have at least a rudimentary orientation on that thing in your head. So stay with us for a few paragraphs.

In terms of macro anatomy, the brain has two hemispheres (the left side and right side). Most of you are probably familiar with the overgeneralized idea that the right hemisphere is the center of the creative mind while the left hemisphere is responsible for the logical mind.

The brain has three layers. In their book *Neuromarketing* (2007), Patrick Renvoise and Christophe Morin purposefully oversimplify the characterization of the functioning of the three brain layers. The three layers are shown in Figure 8.3. They say the top layer, also known as the cortex, thinks rationally. The mid-layer is concerned with emotions and feelings. The deep layer triggers decisions.

The cortex (that is, the top layer) is also divided into four lobes (see Figure 8.4): the frontal, parietal, temporal, and occipital lobes. The frontal lobe is located in the forehead area, and is responsible for higher-level thinking. It's the headquarters, if you like. The parietal lobe is located just behind the crown of the head, and is responsible for associating sensory information (think market research). The occipital lobe is located in the protruding back portion of the head. It is responsible for our visual processing. The temporal lobe is located at the side of the head, and is responsible for hearing and speech. It's our call center.

There are two type of neuronal matter, gray and white matter. Neurons are the basic type of cells in the brain, which transmit information in the nervous system. Gray matter makes up about 77 percent of our brains. Gray matter means there is a thick density of neuron bodies indicating more processing power. White matter means there are more of the tentacles of neurons which carry information to and from the neuron. So gray matter is equated to operations and white matter is distribution.

While brain maps have been produced and can be relied upon, none of our brains is an exact copy of anyone else's. There are always anomalies and special characteristics, which make it very difficult to pinpoint an exact location in any one person's brain. What good would any map be if you could pinpoint your exact location with accuracy? Neuroscience gets around this particular problem through the use of stereotaxic positioning. Stereotaxis is brain geometry. It uses a Cartesian coordinate system – the same system that is used to map the stars and planets. Stereotaxis is a crucial to any brain mapping or surgery. Without it we are guessing where any particular structure is in an individual's head. Understanding neuroexperience is not possible without stereotaxic positioning.

That bit of neuroanatomy highlight is all we need to orient ourselves as we shed light on the goldmine areas of the customer brain. Remember, what we ultimately want to know is what parts of the brain can be mined for value like a goldmine. By goldmine, we mean an area of the brain that has been identified as playing a direct role in customer-oriented decision making and attitude formation, especially as it relates to our emotional or subconscious experience. While the whole brain certainly plays a coordinated role in what we do, we are specifically interested in those parts of the brain that control or modulate what we do in the consumer context.

That's the hard bit over with. As we discussed in previous chapters, the Customer Experience is made up of two halves (see Figure 8.5), a conscious rational half and a subconscious emotional half. Most large organizations have become successful by researching and manipulating the factors that tend to weigh in on the rational experience.

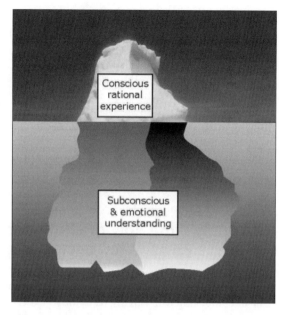

We are now learning how to apply the tools and methodology of neuroscience to unlock the subconscious and emotional side of Customer Experience. The big implication here is that the most valuable nuggets are to be found by shedding light on the non-rational aspects of neuroexperience.

Figure 8.5 The two halves of the Customer Experience

One of the reasons we are beginning to understand the neuroexperience is the explosion of advances in cheaper and more powerful imaging techniques. With these methods a great deal has already been learned. Martin Lindstrom outlines several studies in his book *Buyology* that demonstrate how one of these imaging devices (fMRI) is already being used to understand and in some cases overturn traditionally held beliefs about how we make decisions and what affects our decision making. It is also telling that the 2003 Nobel Prize in medicine was awarded to Paul C. Lauterbur, a chemist, for his contribution in the early 1970s to the invention of MRI. Nobel awards in science and economics are pretty good at indicating which ideas, tools, and techniques are sea changers and will be increasingly applied moving forward.

Recently, all the buzz has surrounded fMRI (functional magnetic resonance imaging). This is a non-invasive brain imaging technique that allows researchers to see the brain processing dynamically. It is more of a video than just a series of photographs. It videos where the brain is using oxygen – clever, huh? So we can ask you to spell "cat" and see where your brain is kicking in to come up with the answer "C A T." The same is done with more sophisticated problems. We can simply present a brand and see if the brain is more excited or less excited. We can have you listen to a call and see what is happening in the brain.

Interestingly, we can get you to fill out a consumer survey and see what the brain was really doing while you were rationalizing your answers. Perhaps you answered one way but your brain told a different story. The ultimate use of all this is that fMRI is our prospector's pan. We are using it to find the neural nuggets of gold.

There are other techniques like EEG (electroencephalogram) that are also helpful. EGG is less specific than fMRI, but it can be portable, allowing it to be used in real-life situations like shopping. fMRI still requires the customer to lie prone in the fMRI scanner. As we advance in computing power and nanotechnology, these limitations will no doubt be overcome. Nonetheless, at this stage, fMRI has proven to be the most useful for prospecting for business-relevant brain gold.

Neuropoly – the holy grail of neuroexperience

Much research has already been done to determine brain functionality, of course. Some of this work allows us to create a *Monopoly*-like board linking certain brain structures to these key emotions. In other words, it is like focusing on buying the most expensive properties on the *Monopoly* board. Imagine that we can begin to put together a map of neural goldmines that are waiting to be prospected. It is still early days for such an approach to be considered absolute, but we can certainly begin to get an idea of which areas of the brain are the ripest for neuro-experience harvesting.

In *Monopoly* real-estate properties are listed on the playing field, showing their value. Similarly, we can create a "Neuropoly" board with reference to brain real estate. Our playing field then will have 20 spaces, each one corresponding to the Emotional Signature® emotions we have discussed in previous chapters. The emotions are the value indicators. The clear emotions (in Figure 8.6) drive value and the shaded emotions destroy value.

Our aim is to attempt to locate some evidence of activity that a particular brain structure, process, or chemical is closely linked with a particular emotion. It might sound simple, but the brain is extremely complex, and most functions are duplicated to some degree several times over. As a result, we cannot pinpoint exactly what part of the brain is responsible for which emotion. Nevertheless, the ultimate aim is to find the part of the brain that is closely linked to that emotion. If we can do this we will have the keys to the subconscious experience. With experience psychology, we can get this by way of proxy. When we get to the point that we can do this via the neuroexperience, we will have a direct-line, unfiltered, and true eagle-eyed view of the source code to the half of the Customer Experience that is most difficult to understand. The illumination of the neuroexperience will maximize our

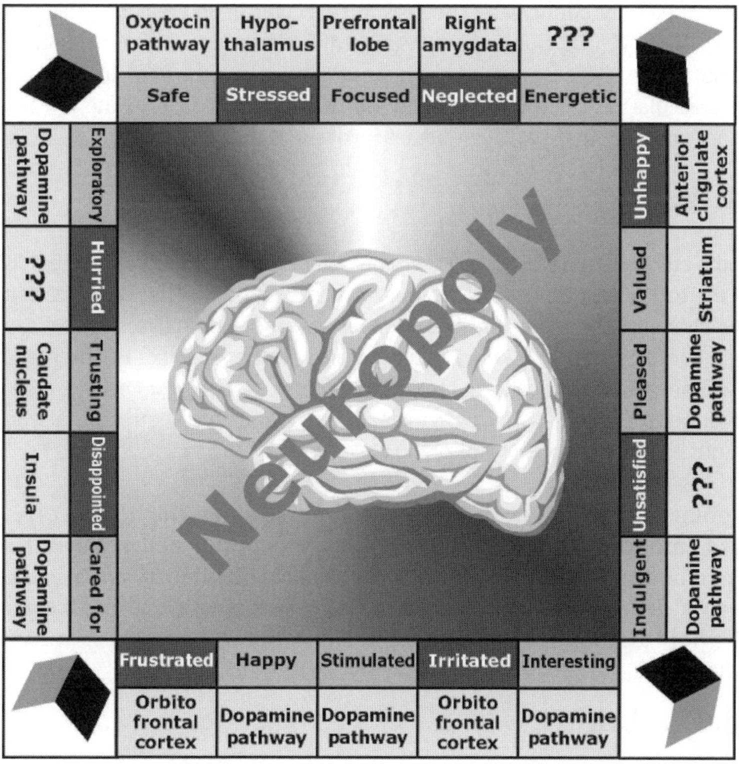

Figure 8.6 Neuropoly

	Oxytocin pathway	Hypo-thalamus	Prefrontal lobe	Right amygdata	???	
	Safe	Stressed	Focused	Neglected	Energetic	
Dopamine pathway / Exploratory						Unhappy / Anterior cingulate cortex
??? / Hurried						Valued / Striatum
Caudate nucleus / Trusting						Pleased / Dopamine pathway
Insula / Disappointed						Unsatisfied / ???
Dopamine pathway / Cared for						Indulgent / Dopamine pathway
	Frustrated	Happy	Stimulated	Irritated	Interesting	
	Orbito frontal cortex	Dopamine pathway	Dopamine pathway	Orbito frontal cortex	Dopamine pathway	

ability to drive value for the business, because we will then know what activates the brain in a way that leads to the behaviors and attitudes the business is interested in.

It turns out that with a bit of poetic license, Figure 8.6 gives an idea of what a Neuropoly board might look like, based on some current studies. Again, none of the brain areas listed on our Neuropoly board have been determined to be specifically responsible for an associated emotion. They have however been implicated in playing a role in that emotion. The association of the emotions to these specific brain systems is a gross oversimplification.

Gemma Calvert, a leading neuromarketer, states that:

A hundred years of neuroscience with brain damaged patients, who have lesions in particular areas and they can't do various tasks, have identified what different bits of the brains do and what they are specialized for. In addition more invasive work in primates with electrodes have given very clear specificity about what the cells in particular brain areas do. This and more than 10,000 publications using fMRI allow us to build a database about when these particular brain areas are active and what their role is in particular task. Then you start to see how different tasks relate to each other and why that particular area is involved in that task.[1]

She goes on to state that:

some emotions have been very well characterized in the monkey. Some cells in the top layer code the pleasantness in a linear fashion. The more pleasant the stimulus, the more that brain real estate becomes active and this can be quantified. We also know there are areas rather specific. For example, there are areas that deal with craving for nicotine, craving for cocaine, areas involved in disgust, dislike or actually that respond to something that you ought to like but you are not going to let yourself say so.

The point here is that the evidence is coming in about the neural correlates of emotions. Eventually we will know the specific neural correlates of the emotions that drive and destroy value. Suffice it to say that the closer we get to pinpointing those neural goldmines, the closer we get to the holy grail of neuroexperience – Neuropoly.

Share of brain

Neuropoly is the holy grail of neuroexperience. Neuropoly occurs when the organization effectively monopolizes the areas of the brain known to drive and destroy the Customer Experience. In neuroexperience terms, neuropoly then represents a 100 percent share of brain. Share

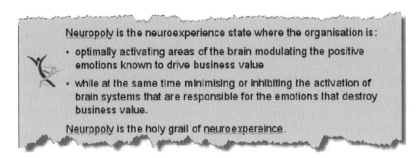

Neuropoly is the neuroexperience state where the organisation is:

- optimally activating areas of the brain modulating the positive emotions known to drive business value
- while at the same time minimising or inhibiting the activation of brain systems that are responsible for the emotions that destroy business value.

Neuropoly is the holy grail of neuroexpereince.

Figure 8.7 A definition of neuropoly

---

1   From an intervciew with Steven Walden.

of brain becomes the key metric in neuroexperience. The question is, "How much of the key areas of the brain directly responsible for driving or destroying business value does the organization influence?" The answer, like market share or share of wallet, will inevitably be some percentage less than 100. The key point is that as neuroexperience advances, it will be possible for organizations to literally view or calculate their share of brain.

The idea is that when the neuroexperience tipping point becomes manifest, the new competitive battleground for business will be located on the real estate within our skulls, literally. It is not difficult to see that a new kind of accounting then becomes possible. Accounting is the communication of business results via financial statements and such. Let's call the new type of accounting "neuro-accounting," and define it as the tracking and communication of business results based on share of brain metrics.

Effectively there is a battle for the subconscious mind between brands.

Currently, customer research is based on the black box model where the brain is a known but hidden filter. Experience psychology uses techniques to decipher that filter so that outputs may be estimated. More traditional techniques ask straightforward questions like "Do you like a particular product or service?" Gemma Calvert reports that:

> there are some quite nice examples where people in focus group have said one thing but the brain response [based on fMRI] has shown exactly the opposite. In fact, in one particular case the product we were looking at had actually been launched in another country and failed on the back of focus group data. And there we had exactly the scenario that they would have been facing. We asked our subjects to tell us what they thought of the product. Whether they would buy it or liked it and so forth. And they said " yes it is absolutely fine etc." and ticked all the boxes but the brain said no. With this information at hand you could go back and run further more focus groups or just be more specific about what kind of information you are gathering out of focus groups.[2]

Unlike traditional techniques, neuroexperience focuses on the black box and opens it up for examination (see Figure 8.8). The filter becomes the object of study because in fact the filter is the root cause, the source code of outputs. It is the understanding of the source code that will allow us to better engineer, influence, and more accurately predict customer attitudes and behaviors, because knowing how inputs

---

2   From an interview with Steven Walden.

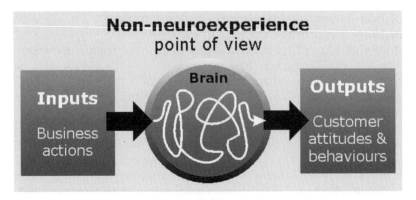

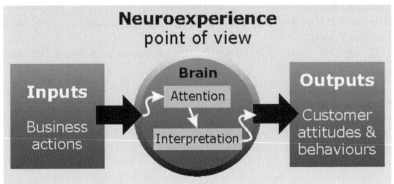

Figure 8.8 Opening up the black box

are processed and lead to outputs is infinitely more powerful than just observing which inputs lead to which outputs.

Consider the following analogy. It is one thing to observe that tall parents tend to have tall children. It is quite another to identify the genetic code for height. In the former case, we can guess that a child might be tall. We would be able to state a rule that if the parents are tall it is likely that the child will be tall. Essentially, what we would have is an after-the-fact rationale to explain the child's height that has already been observed. In the latter case (with an identified genetic code), we can determine whether a child will be tall regardless of the height of the parents. Here we would be able to state a rule that if the child has the "tall" genetic code, then the child will be tall regardless of the parents' height. Furthermore, we can potentially manipulate the genetic code to ensure that a given child is tall.

Neuroexperience falls into the latter category. It allows us to decipher the source code of the Customer Experience. We are literally beginning to map the neuroexperience. With that knowledge, we will be able to build stronger brands, understand exactly what little things we do that make our customers loyal (or defect), and what gets them to part with more of their hard-earned money for our goods and services rather than the competition's. In short, the emerging understanding of neuroexperience will allow a business to more efficiently approach the Holy Grail, neuropoly.

While we are not yet ready to create our Neuropoly game board, neuroscientists have started to explore the world of customer neuro-experience, and the findings are proving interesting. Let's next have a look at a few of these studies and what they say about Customer Experience.

9 A neuroexperience safari – approaching the tipping point

Let us start with a practical application of neuromarketing to show what forward-thinking organizations are doing today.

The Campbell Soup Company employed an approach closely aligned to neuroexperience to redesign its canned soup labeling. The problem Campbell faced is classic. Its condensed soup category is not growing. Campbell wants to sell more soup. Its goal is to increase sales by 2 percent over a two-year period. It has tried every tactic in the book. After all, the Campbell Soup Company has been around for over 100 years. It needed a new way of looking at things, and found it in neuroexperience.

Actually the approach the company took is a biometric one. Biometrics is a first cousin of neuroexperience. Campbell relied on measures that are recognizable from lie detector tests. The volunteers in the research wore vests that measured pupil dilation, skin moisture levels, heart rate, depth and pace of breathing, and posture. The researchers were also able to track their eye movements. This is clearly a practical approach that is very closely aligned with neuroexperience. As we have pointed out, biometrics tell only if a person reacted to something, not whether they liked or disliked something. Nevertheless, if all of the biometrics are spiking, it indicates that some sort of emotional engagement is happening.

In a nutshell, what the researchers found was that there was clear evidence of biometric spiking when Campbell soups were used and discussed in the home, where the soup was associated with warmth and other positive characteristics. However, this spiking all but disappeared in the store aisles. It was clear that Campbell needed to update its packaging.

The newly designed Campbell Soup labels should begin to appear shortly. The big bold red Campbell label will be no more, except for the ever popular and iconic tomato (the inspiration for Andy Warhol's famous pop art), chicken noodle, and cream of mushroom varieties. There will be color coding to help organize the main categories of condensed soups: orange for "taste sensations" and light brown for "classic favorites." The company's logo will be smaller and moved lower so it is not as prominent.

This is a great example of an offshoot of neuroexperience. We wait with interest to see the results. However, as we outlined earlier with the Best Buy example of Twelpforce, Campbell should be applauded for being bold and trying a different approach. It is all well and good doing classic research, but real competitive advantage often comes from the insights provided by looking at your business from new angles.

Now let's take a journey through London. As part of our educational programs, we often take clients out on what we call Customer Experience Safaris. Qaalfa calls it an in-your-face field trip for corporate types. It's the behind-the-scenes story of the best (and worst) practices explained at the point of sale. Colin says it's taking the classroom out onto the street. We take managers into different stores where they have different Customer Experiences. Qaalfa picks up the story:

> I was taking some clients on one of our Customer Experience Safaris where we get people to view the Customer Experience from a more complete perspective. We want them to see begin to appreciate the subconscious and emotional aspects of the experiences. On this occasion, we were walking along Regent Street and Oxford Street – two of the main shopping streets in London. This area also includes Piccadilly Circus and Leicester Square, which are roughly equivalent to Broadway and Times Square in New York.
>
> We got to experience England's largest toy store, Hamleys, with its interactive hands-on experience. There's Apple with another take on the hands-on experience. There's National Geographic and the aromatic Lush. There's the friendly efficiency of Pret A Manger, a fast-food sandwich store, and the consistency of McDonald's along with the ever-present Starbucks. As we were walking through the various experiences, providing insights into why certain experiences left us with the impressions they do, and how these affect people's eventual buying decisions. I began to ponder how these safari experiences might be explained via neuroexperience.

It will not be long before a neuroexperience safari is a practical reality. Instead of simply visiting the stores and then debriefing our clients, as with the current safari, we will run through the experiences while the participants are being brain scanned in some way. The ultimate would be to use a portable fMRI scanner. Short of that, perhaps the idea will be to use portable EEG. It was explained in Chapter 8 that the benefit of EEG is that is can be portable, but it is not as specific as fMRI in the information it provides.

Another possibility might be to have participants walk the experiences while wearing spy cams. These video cameras would capture the experience of the participant in situ. Later, these images could be played back to them while they are being scanned by fMRI. This is not quite as good as being scanned live, but it is a close second. At any rate, the point is that neuroexperience safaris in some form are possible now.

Neuro-this and neuro-that

Even though neuroexperience is in its infancy, the excitement is brewing and pioneers have started to apply neuroscience to the world of the customer. Why? They want to understand:

- the source code of our decision making, good and bad
- how we process information – consciously and subconsciously
- what really influences us
- the fallacy of the rational mindset and the power and source of our irrationality
- the laws of effective customer interaction (based on source code processing rather than black box observation).

In a nutshell, neuroscience is becoming pervasive in its effect on business. "Neuro" as a prefix is becoming a useful concept for many areas of practical, often unexpected, application. Marco Roth points out that the neuronovel is gaining in popularity, and is quickly becoming a new strain of novel.[1] He points out that since 1997, the psychological or confessional novel has been transformed into the neurological novel.

The neuronovel is evidence that neuro-this and neuro-that are seeping into almost every facet of our lives. Consider this: it was not long ago that the anything neurological was for "brain surgeons" only (that is, off limits to those of us who are less than absolutely brilliant). Society in general has become better educated on disorders of the brain. Now, we often look to for neurological explanations for strange behavior.

In the past, people would commonly say that a deranged person was just "crazy" or perhaps even "evil." We now accept or even look for underlying neurological disorders to explain why some neighbor or co-worker who had never caused any problem suddenly went berserk. When we hear of someone going "postal," society now needs to know whether there is some form of brain disorder that caused this aberrant behavior.

In the United States, perhaps it was the infamous 1966 University of Texas tower massacre that brought the brain and the effects of its

---

1 Marco Roth, The rise of the Neuronovel, *n+1*, Issue 8, October 2009, http://www.nplusonemag.com/rise-neuronovel (accessed May 18, 2010)

dysfunction so clearly to the public's eye. Qaalfa grew up in Texas, and he tells us that massacre is still part of the psyche there. Student Charles Whitman went on a rampage at the school, before eventually barricading himself atop the school's 307 foot observation tower and acting as a sniper. In the end he killed 14 people and injured 32 others. He was from an upper-middle-class family, excelled at academic studies, and was well liked by his peers and neighbors. So why did he switch so dramatically? His autopsy showed that he had a massive cancerous brain tumor. Unfortunately, there are of course many examples of this, and society has come to appreciate the link between neuroscience and behavior. Indeed, we have in many instances started to be fascinated by it. This fascination can be observed in a variety of ways.

One interesting example is the neuronovel. According to Marco Roth:

> the neuronovel represents a cultural sea change and follows a cultural (and, in psychology proper, a disciplinary) shift away from environmental and relational theories of personality back to the study of brains themselves, as the source of who we are.

An example is Ian McEwan's 1997 novel *Enduring Love*, which highlights de Clérambault's syndrome. Clérambault's syndrome is a type of delusion in which the affected person believes that another person is in love with him or her. The illness often occurs during psychosis, especially in patients with schizophrenia. Interestingly a fictional case prepared by a fictional psychiatrist is included in the book, along with a useful bibliography about the illness. When a popular novel includes a medical case history, you know the general level of neuro-acceptance is high.

Enduring Love was made into a movie in 2004. However, the real neuroexperience revolution in movies is not in the content on the screen. It's in how the movies are developed.

Part of our London-based Customer Experience Safari takes us through Leicester Square, with all of its cinemas. The neuroexperience of the cinema is here in the form of neurocinema. Peter Katz produced the world's first neurocinema, the horror film *Pop Skull* (2007). The basis of neurocinema is understanding how the brain responds to scenes in order to make better movies.

Let us explain. A horror movie is all about fear. As viewers, we want to feel that fear. Peter Katz recognized that real fear occurs via the neuroexperience. Movie goers are not consciously in tune with their fear levels throughout a movie with enough specificity to remember or know what their relative reactions to specific events in a movie were. So asking to rate them on a scale of 1 to 10 how scary they found scenes leaves movie makers with a gaping hole in their understanding. Viewers are not often able to pinpoint the exact stimuli that caused them to feel fearful. It may be that the most memorable thing in a scene was not necessarily the most frightening. Neurocinema gets around this problem by looking directly at the source code of fear in people's brains.

It is known that one particular piece of the physical brain (the amygdala) is highly involved in feelings of fear, disgust, and anger – the emotions you want to elicit in high doses in a horror film. In other words, we no longer have the filter of a black box brain to contend with. Instead, we can look directly at the source code in the brain to create a horror film that is closer to neuropoly. Neuropoly in horror neurocinema would be optimal engagement of the brain while maximizing the feelings of fear.

What's exciting is that fMRI brain scans of a viewer showed lots of appropriate activity during the movie's scary scenes. The brain and especially the amygdala lit up like a Christmas tree out of fear. This activity was pinpointed to the frame, the exact scene and action that registered the response. For instance, "The scariest moment in Scene 1 came when the hand reaches further around the corner." It is that precise. How can any focus group be that exact in locking down the exact moment that they felt fear?

The fMRI scans of a movie viewer looking at scenes from the movie were analyzed. The results were startling and very telling. The researchers were looking for lots of activity in the amygdala, because lots of amygdala activation means "money shot" in horror films. Through analyzing the real-time viewing of the scene, Katz and his colleagues were able to pinpoint the exact moment that is considered most scary, even when the viewer could only say that the entire scene was scary. In other words, if Katz found that a particular scene was not as scary as he had hoped, he could compare what he thought was frightening to what actually was frightening.

The most counterintuitive finding was that the most visually inter-esting point in one particular scene was the least scary. It had all the signs of being scary. A man was snatched and bundled into a side room, and right afterwards viewers saw a body on the floor (presumably this man's body), covered by a white sheet, in an eerie cold room, with the camera slowly approaching and ominous music playing in the back-ground. But actually the scariest point in the scene was simply a man's arm slowly reaching around a corner at the top of a staircase. It's just a nondescript arm slowly emerging from around a corner. It is likely that the viewer pointed out the least fear-inducing part of this scene (the snatched man) as the most fear-inducing simply because it is the most memorable.

When asked whether there really is a big difference between the results researchers get from traditional focus groups and those they get from neurocinema research, Dr. David Hubbard, a board-certified neurologist who was the leading neurologist on the *Pop Skull* neuro-cinema project, recounts the following:

> Recently we scanned a subject whose brain showed only little reaction to a scary scene. On her questionnaire she dutifully wrote "I liked it," "very scary," although she confided to the scan technician that actually she found it boring, as did her brain. Besides the problem of focus group subjects saying what they think the interviewer wants to hear, a bigger problem is that they don't remember what they saw a minute ago. When you ask them which scene they liked best, they can seldom remember. FMRI eliminates both these problems. We can see directly which scenes excite which regions of the brain every one to two seconds, whether the subject is aware of it, or says so or not.[2]

What are the results? *Pop Skull* is a low-budget horror movie so it is not likely to make it to a major-release cinema of the type generally found in Leicester Square. It is more likely to be found at an art house cinema. Nevertheless, it has received glowing reviews. One review said it is "a text book example of what you can do on a budget if you're smart enough."[3]

Pop Skull is a first find in neurocinema. More are sure to follow as directors and producers learn how to make the best use of the neuro-experience. Think of the power of understanding in that level of detail what actions drive value in your Customer Experience. If you know that you want to evoke in a customer the feeling that you value them, what very detailed actions, like this example of the arm moving, would do this for you?

The neurocinematic approach may soon be applied to comedies as well. Joseph Moran of Dartmouth College preformed fMRI brain scans on volunteers while they watched TV comedies. He found that areas of the brain that are typically involved in language comprehension and the ability to shift attention were heavily activated. a particular pattern of neural activity in response to funny jokes.

Other researchers have found that there is secondary activity in the limbic system which plays a key role in establishing reward and pleasure. This secondary response may kick in when we "get the joke." It is not difficult to see how a neurocinematic comedy director could use this

---

2 Curtis Silver, Neurocinema aims to change the way movies are made, *Wired*, September 2009.

3 Todd Brown, review of Pop Skill, *Twitch*, December 27, 2007 (http://twitchfilm. net/reviews/2007/12/pop-skull-reiew.php).

information to understand when and if the audience gets the joke. The timing between the first comprehension phase and the secondary "got it" phase could help pace a comedy for maximal effect, or tell the director whether jokes are too difficult for the audience to make out.

The Leicester Square portion of the safari might not look all that different on the surface, but behind many of the films in the neuroexperience age will be neurocinematic filmmaking. I envision that many of the cinema billboards and rolling credits will include something along the lines of "produced via Neurocinemascope." Such a label will mean as much to us in the future as Dolby, Imax, or 3D does now.

Applied neurocinema, or neurocinemascope, or whatever it will be called, will not guarantee box office success on its own. Nevertheless, while there are other factors involved, optimized feelings of horror are surely one of the key factors in a horror film's success. Neurocinema is not just an interesting academic experiment. It will in the future help movies achieve box office success.

It is not a stretch to see that the neurocinema concept could easily be applied to many things in this "neuro-this and that" world. For example:

- viewing websites (neuro-usability studies), where instead of viewing a movie the subject searches for information on a website
- brand impressions (neurobranding), where the subject looks at advertising or is presented with various products or packaging (as you might do in an implicit attitude test)
- taste tests (neuro-taste tests).

What has all this to do with the Customer Experience? Imagine that you could do the same with your Customer Experience. In time, you should be able to have a customer walk through your customer journey and view their neuroexperience as it happens. You will be able to see whether they really trust the company, or are frustrated by the experience, and by how much. These neuroexperience-based metrics would be actionable. This research can be just as actionable for you in your business as it is for film directors in neurocinema. So like neurocinema you could construct your new experience to take away the frustration and increase the levels of feeling cared for and so on. Given that level of actionability, it is not much of a step to suggest that managers could also be bonused and incentivized on this as a key performance indicator. Very powerful indeed!

Consider how the bright lights and digital billboards of Piccadilly Circus could be optimized via neuromarketing. Piccadilly Circus is London's rough equivalent to Times Square. It is a marketing mecca of gigantic advertisements and flashing billboards. In some sense, the neuroexperience safari of the future might look a bit like the scene from *Minority Report* we mentioned on page 127. Some day we might get that "John Anderton" experience, so that as we walk through Piccadilly Circus, the billboards might change based on the collective average of the multiple real-time scans that are taking place at street level. It's a dream for now, but that could be the neuroexperience-enhanced Piccadilly Circus of the future.

As we continue our Customer Experience Safari, we leave Piccadilly Circus and turn into Regent Street. A little way down we hit the Apple Store. Apple has made a name for itself by being the hipster computer company. It's Steve Jobs versus Bill Gates. Of course, Apple has great products like the iPod, iPhone, and the Mac, but it also has something else – it's cool. IBM was never really cool. I don't think Microsoft was ever cool. Nor did Dell did promote coolness, or Sir Alan Sugar's Amstrad in the United Kingdom. These companies might be, or have been, extremely profitable, but cool? Umm ... no. I find it difficult to think of many more high-tech manufacturers that are cool. Sony at one time had it, but it has almost lost it. What makes a company cool?

Steve Quartz performed a neurobranding study of different products using fMRI. Each of the products (Apple, Audi, Christian Dior, and so on) shared high brand equity and was considered "cool."[4] He found that the brain area of interest is in the cortex just behind the forehead. This area of the brain is called Brodmann's area 10. Quartz suggests that this indicates that "cool products" are being processed in terms of their ability to enhance social image. Not exactly a mind-blowing thought, you might think, but he also found that these "cool products" activate the nucleus accumbens, a key reward center in the brain. It is thought to play an important role in reward, laughter, pleasure, addiction, fear, and the placebo effect. This reward center is heavily involved in addictions (for instance, to heroin). So an implication is that high brand equity is a kind of addiction. Quartz's study is an academic one, but it gives a clue to the power of neuromarketing for organizations. Unfortunately for businesses, unlike addiction, coolness can cease when its ability to enhance social image wanes.

Apple designs social status into its products, not just high functionality. Quartz's neurobranding study gives us proof that it is the social enhancement that makes Apple cool. In case you are wondering why you needed a neurobranding study to tell you the "obvious," consider this. With neurobranding, a company can determine its "coolness" before the kids tell you whether it's cool nor not. It gives you a hard

---

4   Kermit Pattison, What makes a product cool, *Fast Company*, November 21, 2007 <http://www.fastcompany.com/articles/2007/11/interview-quartz.html> (accessed June 1, 2010).

measure of coolness, and a way to get at the magnitude of "coolness" based on measures of brain functioning.

The next stop on our journey is Starbucks. Starbucks provides a great example of Customer Experience. It is generally consistent and deliberate in its Customer Experience. It does many things right. That's obvious, as Starbucks has grown to literally be the "third place" for many people. Home is first, work is second, and Starbucks is third. Interestingly, Starbucks could also claim to be the second office. It is a core resource for freelancers, and provides an extra meeting space for those in over-cramped offices.

There is no doubt that Starbucks' vision and philosophy mean that the company welcomes people to use its spaces as it were their own, but one fMRI study provides another interesting take on why Starbucks is a successful third place and second office.

Researchers Lawrence Williams and John Bargh gave their subjects either hot or iced coffee to drink, then asked them to rate other people's personalities.[5] The raters were only given a printed profile of the people whose personality they were rating. Those who had been given the hot coffee rated the personalities significantly higher in terms of warmth than those who had been given iced coffee. Hot and cold temperature stimuli trigger an area of the brain that is associated with making people non-trusting and uncooperative.

So perhaps one of the subconscious key success factors to the Starbucks phenomenon (especially for business people) is that it helps trigger an area of the brain that enhances our perception that others around us are warm and trustworthy. This is great for business deals, negotiations, and introductions. When you pair this with the Starbucks vision of being open for use as a meeting space, you have a recipe for success.

While we may have made a case for the success of a hot drinks café over say a smoothie bar as a third place, we have not really addressed why Starbucks has succeeded over its competition. On Regent Street, as elsewhere, Starbucks faces formidable competition. On and around Regent Street there are outlets for Costa Coffee, Coffee Republic, Café Nero, Café Amore, Carluccio's Café, and more. It is clear that Starbucks does not have any warmer coffee than these others. McDonald's has already tried the piping hot coffee thing and was infamously sued when someone spilled the hot drink on themselves some years back. In fact, many people will argue that Starbucks does not have the best coffee. So what is it about Starbucks that makes it special out of the hot drinks outlets?

---

5 Lawrence E. Williams and John A. Bargh, Experiencing physical warmth promotes interpersonal warmth, Science, October 24, 2008, issue, 322(5901), pp. 606–7.

We have not seen a study specific to Starbucks yet, but the choice between Pepsi and Coke is similar to that between the various cafés' coffees. These firms are hypercompetitive, and there is no discernible quality difference. Clive Thompson of the *New York Times* reported on one of the seminal neuromarketing studies where Read Montague and team performed a classic taste test between Coke and Pepsi.[6] He wanted to know why Coke was so appealing if it really did not taste better than Pepsi. You may recall that in the now famous Pepsi TV commercials, subjects usually chose Pepsi over Coke in a blind taste test.[7] Montague found that Pepsi did indeed produce greater activation in another of the brain's reward centers, part of the striatum. Interestingly he found that the brain reward center activity of Pepsi lovers drinking Pepsi was five times that of Coke lovers drinking Coke. In other words, Pepsi is apparently five times as rewarding for Pepsi lovers as Coke is for Coke lovers based on taste alone. This corroborated the findings shown in the TV commercials.

This creates an interesting question, though. If the Pepsi taste is so rewarding, why then is it not generally the market leader? Montague took the study further to answer this question. In the next round, he unblinded the study for the tasters, and told them what they were about to taste. Coke won under these conditions: almost everyone now chose Coke. Importantly for us, the brain activity of the participants also changed! This time other areas were activated – the same brain areas that were activated in the Quartz study on high brand equity products, where their activity in response to those products was interpreted as enhancing social value leading to coolness. Similarly Montague interprets the activation of this region in the unblinded taste test as a signal that the tasters were now processing more of the branding and relying on memories and other impressions to influence them.

What Montague demonstrated was the ability of brand to override taste (or the straightforward rational aspect of an experience) in choice decisions. What's interesting here is that this could help answer the question of whether to favor marketing budget or product innovation budget. If you are paying attention, in business terms, Montague might have just provided a neuroexperience approach to answer the question "Where should we invest: product promotion or product innovation?" In this case, marketing could make the case that its efforts override those of the guys in product innovation. This development

---

6   Clive Thompson, There's a sucker born in every medial prefrontal cortex, *New York Times*, October 2003: http://www.nytimes.com/2003/10/26/magazine/26BRAINS.html?ex=1068147831&ei=1&en (accessed May 18, 2010).

7   An 1983 example of the Pepsi challenge TV ad from Australia can be seen on http://www.youtube.com/watch?v=v7lw_vhxtNc (accessed May 18, 2010).

of this thinking and practice would be another brick in the still-to-be-developed space of neuroaccounting (or neuro business cases).

How does that relate to Starbucks, Costa, and the rest of the cafés? It suggests that Starbucks' strategy of being the third place is likely to have helped drive its success. As people incorporated Starbucks into their daily lives as meeting point, chill-out spot, extra meeting space, and so on, customers were steadily activating that social enhancement area of the brain. This strategy effectively helps Starbucks' customers process more branding and associate more memories and other impressions to influence their choices. Some of Starbucks' competitors do not want to be anything like a third space (for instance, Carluccio's). This chain wants to be a place for people to have a high-end cup of coffee or meal. Others like Café Amore are closer to a local shop. It could not be that third space because its outlets simply do not exist in as many convenient spots as Starbucks. However, Nero in London is in the same geographic realm as Starbucks. Essentially, Starbucks is the Coke to Nero's Pepsi.

Just around the corner there are several grocery stores to visit. These stores are like any you might be familiar with, but neuroexperience is starting to shape the look of the products that sit on the shelves. Executives at PepsiCo's Frito-Lay (crisps as they are called in the United Kingdom, or chips as they are known in the United States) unit used neuromarketing to test commercials, products, and packaging in the United States and overseas.[8] Their previous research showed that women in particular feel guilty at snacking. To add insult to injury, they knew that women snack more than men, but they were not snacking on more Frito-Lay snacks. Men eat more salty snacks than women, so it is important that Frito-Lay minimizes the guilt women might feel while they are in purchase decision mode, shopping in the aisles of stores.

The starting point for Frito-Lay was not the packaging itself. It was the age-old question of gender differences. Frito-Lay wanted to know how women's and men's brains differed – which brain real estate was activated differentially for men and women. Frito-Lay went straight to academic neuroscience on gender differences, and found that areas of women's brains responsible for communication and emotions were more developed than men's. So its researchers decided to design packaging prototypes that were a bit more complex and generated warmer feelings than they might have done if the packaging had been solely for men.

Frito-lay needed a way to determine which of its prototype designs

---

8   Stephanie Clifford, Frito-Lay tries to enter the minds (and lunch bags) of women, *New York Times*, February 24, 2009 <http://www.nytimes.com/2009/02/25/business/media/25adco.html> (accessed June 2, 2010).

produced the least guilt. It makes sense then that the goal was to produce packaging that waylays the guilt as much as possible. But how do you understand what is it about packaging that makes customers feel more or less guilt? Could Frito-Lay have expected a valuable answer if researchers had simply asked customers to tell them how guilty they felt in focus groups? The answer is a resounding "No." So Frito-Lay turned to neuroexperience for the answers.

In the end the researchers discovered that matte beige bags of potato chips picturing potatoes and other "healthy" ingredients in the snack don't trigger an area of the brain associated with feelings of guilt as much as shiny yellow bags with pictures of chips. Frito-Lay then switched out of shiny packaging in the United States.

Again, think how this could apply to your organization's Customer Experience. Do you understand what is happening at this level of detail in your Customer Experience? Perhaps you should.

If we continue on with our safari and go just a tad further afield from Regent Street over to the King's Road, we will reach Warr's Harley-Davidson store. Warr's is Europe's oldest Harley dealership. Normally when we speak of Harley-Davidson, you'll hear about how Harley is the flagship brand to demonstrate how a business can become part of its customers' lifestyle. Becoming a literal part of the customer's life and lifestyle is the ultimate loyalty guarantee. Few brands can claim to have such a deep connection with their customers. As evidence, Harley lifestylers have branded themselves with the Harley tattoo. There are one or two other brands that have that kind of attachment with more than just a few of their customers: Disney, Nike, and Apple are prime examples. We have already heard what makes a brand like Apple cool, and that this can be measured through neuroexperience. The obvious question is, "Is there a neuroexperiential gauge for loyalty"?

Gemma Calvert answered just this question in a study she conducted for Hakuhodo – Japan's second largest advertising agency.[9] The company wanted to know what loyalty looks like in the brain, and how it might be different for a football team like Gamba Osaka than for Harley-Davidson. Two groups of subjects were scanned: half of them Harley-Davidson owners, the other half followers of Gamba Osaka. The responses were fascinating.

The scans of Gamba Osaka fans showed that their neuroresponse is similar to that of customers of Coke or Pepsi. Harley-Davison customers' neuroresponse was altogether different! They processed Harley-Davidson like an experience! That is, Harley-Davison produced

---

9   Details of Calvert's study can be found in "Findings from a Neuroscience-Based fMRI Polot Study Report Announced," www.neuroscience.co.uk/docs/Hakuhodo-press-release-2009.pdf.

similar activations to those seen in someone planning a trip. Harley-Davidson's neuroactivation showed that its loyal customers were connecting differently than loyal customers of Gamba Osaka. These two types of loyalty were identified in their neuroexperience.

Gamba Osaka (like Pepsi or Coke) is a battling brand. "Battling brands" attempt to occupy the same place on expensive brain real estate as their competitors. The battle for this brain real estate forces the brain to choose a winner. The neuroresponse of Gamba Osaka was detrimental to competitor teams' activations – there was a battle in the brain for activity, and Gamba Osaka won for its own fans. The net result is that battling brands need to expend lots of effort to maintain their prime brain address. We have previously mentioned how Coke uses its marketing might to hang on to its dominant position in the cola war.

Brands like Harley-Davidson (and we venture to guess Disney) are "positioned brands." Their space is known and does not compete with other brands in the same category. In other words, Harley-Davidson occupies a different space from, say, Honda. In fact, many of the Harley-Davidson bike owners also had Hondas. In other words Harley owns the deed to its brain real estate. It has its neural land fenced in and well marked. The fact that it has neighbors (such as Honda and Yamaha) in the same general area is of little concern. Unlike Gamba Osaka, Harley's brain activation was not detrimental to the neuroresponse to "competitive" brands like Honda. Of course, Harley certainly must mend its fences and settle land disputes here and there, but for all intensive purposes everyone knows which brain real estate is Harley's.

It is important to point out that both types of loyalty can be equally strong. Behaviorally, the loyalty can look the same even though the neuroexperience is different. The implication for businesses is that they can determine whether they have brain real estate to themselves or face a constant battle for ownership. Through tracking fMRI studies a battling brand could tell if it was continuing to win those battles, and by how much. A positioned brand could tell if its fenced position needed mending, and by how much. Of course, any business can wait until the neuroexperience makes itself evident in behavior (for instance, through customer attrition). But as so many former businesses have witnessed, waiting until the pain is felt on the financial statements can often mean it is too late to act with authority. By that time the business can simply be treading water, trying to stay afloat. Neuroexperience provides a powerful new lens by which the business can view itself in the mind's eye of the customer.

The application of neuroscience to business will continue to take hold, especially as methods and technology improve. The tipping point is on this side of the horizon. Already studies have been commissioned by branding powerhouses to better understand how to improve their positioning and win in tightly contested markets. There are plenty of interesting customer experience questions to be answered.

One of the stores that is typically profiled in the London safaris is John Lewis, a leading UK department store. There is something special about John Lewis. In fact, Qaalfa in particular has been on television several times talking about the generally exceptional Customer Experience John Lewis provides. The Oxford Street store has been consistent with its experience over the last several years. The funny thing is that it is difficult to put your finger exactly what it does that's so special. This is not the most flash store, and its product selection is not so different from what you might find elsewhere. It doesn't have animatronics and dancers all about the place. It is a regular department store on the surface. It doesn't really carry the range of high-end designer wear you might find as a matter of course at say Harrods, or have the hip feel of say Selfridges. Nevertheless, there is something that just works at John Lewis. We always ask the safari participants to have a deep investigatory look around and report what they think is John Lewis's secret.

They usually come back with not too much. They have difficulty finding or spotting anything auspicious in the experience. The reason is that they are all looking for a big "wow" or something that dramatically stands out in the experience. But there is nothing that specifically dominates your attention or captures the imagination while shopping at John Lewis.

People eventually point out that John Lewis is a partnership rather than a limited company or corporation. The store staff are part owners of the business. This is a major driving force for its Customer Experience success, but if that were the end of the story, its worth to this book would not be worth the ink I have just used. There are not too many large businesses out there ready to change their ownership structure to improve the Customer Experience. The lesson of the John Lewis experience is that there is a subconscious experience at work.

As customers we might interpret it as a gut feeling, but what is really behind the John Lewis experience from the customer's point of view? Neuroexperience would offer clues as to what is at the core of the John Lewis experience. Any competitor of John Lewis would want to know exactly what it is about the John Lewis service that resonates with customers – what it is that drives so much trust when there is nothing readily apparent on the surface of things. A neuroexperiential investigation would answer this.

In the safaris the focus is primarily on the brand and the Customer Experience. The few studies we have highlighted are really about getting businesses to better understand this and adjust their offering for competitive advantage. Another main branch of neuroexperience is better understanding of how customers make decisions, especially when those decisions are difficult to make: for example when there is risk involved, or when people must choose between two great options. There are three basic types of risk (also known as dissonance) decisions:

- Approach–approach: when you must choose between two or more rewarding options. For example, you are deciding where to go on a trip of a lifetime, which might be either a cruse on the Amazon river or a Kenyan safari.
- Approach–avoidance: when a single option has both positive and negative aspects associated with it. For example, this is the dissonance a person trying to lose weight might feel when deciding whether to have that rich and delicious chocolate dessert.
- Avoidance–avoidance: when you must choose between two punishing options. For example, you decide whether to visit the dentist or live with a mild toothache.

Neuroeconomics is a growing field of study that is mapping the understanding of when a customer will decide to take one option over the other under dissonant conditions. Neuroeconomics is much more about working out the conscious and subconscious rules customers use in their decision making. Most often customers are not aware of these rules, and could not state what they were even if they tried.

As with all of neuroexperience, neuroeconomics illuminates the source code of our decision making. If businesses understood these decision-making rules, they could then better align themselves to the approach customers take when they decide to:

- stay or leave
- buy more or less
- buy for the first time or not.

This is the realm of neuroeconomics, and will be explored in the next chapter.

Figure 9.1 describes, very simply, the end game of customer experience. The top bar, "Customer Expectations," represents the experience the customer would like to receive. This may or may not be grounded in reality. If that bar is set too high, nothing a business can do will satisfy the customer. If the bar is set too low, the customer might never opt to have the experience in the first place. Where the bar is actually set depends on advertising, word-of-mouth, previous experiences with the business or related businesses, the news of the day, and so on.

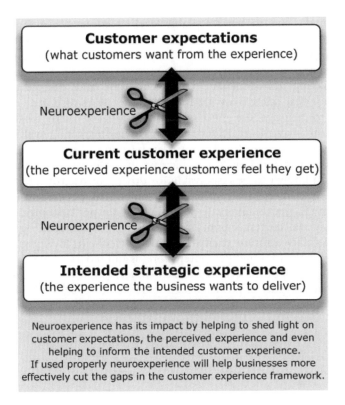

Figure 9.1 The end game of customer experience

The bottom bar, "Intended Strategic Experience," is the experience the business has said it will deliver. Often this is interpreted as the brand. In the best of worlds, the intended strategic experience should be informed by customer expectations but not absolutely driven by them. Why? Because customers might have unrealistic expectations, or the business might not have the capacity or will to deliver certain kinds of experiences. Ultimately, the decision is the business's.

The middle bar, "Current Customer Experience," is the actual experience the business delivers as perceived in the customer's eye (or more accurately, in the customer's brain). Many companies get confused on this one. They assume that a traditional mystery shopping paradigm tells them the experience the customer gets. Sadly, this is generally not the case. Those programs usually tell you whether policy and procedure are being followed, but not too much about the actual Customer Experience.

The goal in Customer Experience is to manage the distances

between the bars within acceptable levels. Neuroexperience will play a crucial role in helping business do so by bringing quantifiable clarity to the top two bars, "Customer Expectations" and "Current Customer Experience."

Marketing departments (and accounting and finance departments for that matter) are always looking for ways to prove (in other words, to quantify) the effect marketing budget is having (that is, the return on investment (ROI)). Perhaps neuromarketing will provide the ultimate answer. It will some day be possible to show that that X marketing spend results in Y increase in some particular brain area activation known to be responsible for driving or destroying value for business. Or alternatively, it might be shown that a Y percent increase in activity in that brain area is worth X amount per customer. Neuro-experience (as currently popularized through neuromarketing) makes this possibility a future reality. Frederick Reichheld, loyalty guru and co-developer of the net promoter score, is quoted as saying that "If a company could turn 5% more of its customers into loyalists, with hooks into their amygdalas, profits would increase 25–100% a customer."[10] This is effectively a marketing department's neuropoly.

---

10 Frederick Reichheld quoted in Tim Manners, "Where's the loyalty," *Fast Company*, January 10, 2005, <http://www.fastcompany.com/resources/marketing/manners/011005.html> (accessed June 2, 2010).

10 The black box in action

Of all the questions neuroexperience can help businesses answer, perhaps none is more crucial than providing clarity about how customers go about making decisions. This involves questions such as:

■ How do customers process marketing information?
■ Why do customers choose certain brands over others?
■ What are the earliest signs that customer expectations are not being met?
■ How do customers perceive the Customer Experience the business provides?
■ How do customers assess risk and reward?

Chapter 9 highlighted a few neuromarketing studies. Neuromarketing is the applied study of how the brain responds to marketing stimuli. The basic marketing stimuli can be interpreted as the Four Ps:

■ Place – where a product or service is sold or delivered.
■ Price – the cost of a product or service.
■ Promotion – the advertising and external communications for a product or service.
■ Product – the actual product or service being promoted.

Neuromarketing has already entered into the vernacular, but how is it being used? Table 10.1 provides a brief and inexhaustive overview of neuromarketing as it relates to the Four Ps. It highlights some of the brain real estate that needs to be engaged in order to ensure success with the Four Ps. Each of the studies profiled provides another clue as to how to construct the Neuropoly game board. We are not yet ready to pinpoint the exact brain real estate that will allow us to construct the game board with authority, but we do know the neural neighborhoods to look in.

Although we can't yet create our Neuropoly game board, researchers are beginning to piece together research to identify the basic building blocks of marketing. We describe the 20 emotions that drive and destroy value for business in our Emotional Signature®. In Emotional

161

Table 10.1 Neuromarketing as it relates to the Four Ps

Product

Question	Method	Set-up	Finding	Brain real estate activated	Source
Is there a neural representation of product attractiveness?	fMRI	Ranking attractiveness of sports cars, limousines, and small cars with scanner and questionnaire	Products that symbolize wealth and prestige lead to a higher activation in areas that are associated with the perception of rewards	Area 34 – the ventral striatum	[1]

Promotion

Question	Method	Set-up	Finding	Brain real estate Activated	Source
What impact does affective advertisement have on neural activity in comparison with cognitive advertisement?	MEG	The subjects watched different commercials with either affective or cognitive content	Cognitive pictures: stronger activation in areas indicating stronger use of working memory. Affective pictures: activation in areas indicating processing of emotional stimuli.	Cognitive pictures: posterior parietal areas and in superior prefrontal cortex. Affective pictures: ventromedial prefrontal cortex, the amygdala and the brain stem.	[2]
Can the perceived attractiveness of an advertisement be associated with specific neural activations?	fMRI	The subjects had to evaluate different advertisements by their attractiveness	Attractive ads lead to a stronger activations in the brain's rewards centers and in areas controlling executive decision making	Nucleus accumbens (part of the striatum), ventromedial posterior frontal cortex	[3]

162

Table 10.1 continued

Price

Question	Method	Set-up	Finding	Brain real estate activated	Source
What impact does the price have on product preferences and neural activity?	fMRI	Products with corresponding price information were presented to subjects who had to make a buy decision	Product preferences activates brain areas shown to be active in the anticipation of gains	Nucleus accumbens is sensitive to product preference. Medial prefrontal cortex reacts to reduced prices. Insula reacts to high prices.	[4]
Is there a neural correlate for the individual willingness to pay?	fMRI	After a wine tasting, subjects had to make buy decisions about wines showing explicit price information	Differential activation in an area playing a role in executive function according to price	Medial prefrontal cortex	[5]

Place

Question	Method	Set-up	Finding	Brain real estate activated	Source
Is it possible to find the "framing effect"* on a neural basis?	fMRI	Loyal and disloyal subjects had to choose between retail brands from which they would prefer to buy an identical garment	Loyal subjects' integrate emotions into decision-making process in a more intense way with favorite brand acting as a rewarding stimulus. Disloyal subjects did not show this effect.	Vetromedial prefrontal cortex	[6]

Note:
* The framing effect is the cognitive bias that is evident when the same option presented to a subject in different settings alters the subject's decisions. For example when the same basic question is answered differently when presented as glass half full versus glass half empty.

Overall source: Adapted from M. Hubert and P. Kenning, A current overview of consumer neuroscience, *Journal of Consumer Behaviour*, 7, 2008/

Table 10.1 continued

In-table sources:
[1] S. Erk, M. Spitzer, A. P. Wunderlich, L. Galley, and H. Walter, Cultural objects modulate reward circuitry, *NeuroReport*, 13(18), 2002.
[2] T. Ambler, A. Ioannides, and S. Rose, Brands on the brain: neuro-images of advertising, *Business Strategy Review*, 11(3), 2000.
[3] P. Kenning, H. Plassmann, W. Kugel Schwindt, A. Pieper, and M. Deppe, Neural correlates of attractive ads, *FOCUS*, 2007.
[4] 7 B. Knutson, S. Rick, G. E. Wimmer, D. Prelee, and G. Loewenstein, Neural predictors of purchase, *Neuron*, 53(1), 2007.
[5] H. Plassman, J. O'Doherty, B. Shiv, and A. Rangel, Marketing actions can modulate neural representations of experienced pleasantness, *Proceedings of National Academy of Sciences of the United States of America*, 105(3), 2008.
[6] H. Plassman, P. Kenning, and D. Ahlert, Why companies should make their customers happy: the neural correlates of customer loyalty, *Advances in Consumer Research*, 34, 2007.

Signature® we identify the emotional drivers and destroyers of business and brand value. Emotional Signature® is an experience psychology technique. Nevertheless, neuroexperience research is in the early days of corroborating our Emotional Signature® findings. The definitive link between any of the specific Emotional Signature® emotions and brain activation will take a while to establish, because several if not many brain structures play a simultaneous role in producing a single felt emotion. Interestingly, neuroexperience research is highlighting the complexity of these linkages, and these have already produced some thinking on what is required at the neural level for branding success.

Tjaco Walvis provides a nice summary of three laws of branding that are derived from neuroexperience investigations. Walvis points out that:

> If strong brands are more valuable at the stock exchange and the three branding laws explain how to create such brands, then the theorem bears promise. With today's rapid advances in neuroscience, it may be possible in coming years to ever more tightly link the micro level of the customer's mental world (where neural associations can be influenced by marketers) to the macro level of companies' financial success and their share process on the stock exchange.[1]

According to Walvis, the three laws of branding are as follows:

■ Brands need to be relevant.
■ Brands need to be coherent.
■ Brands need to be rich.

---

1 Tjaco Walvis, Three laws of branding: Neuroscientific foundations of effective brand building, *Brand Management* 16(3), December 2008.

Brand relevance refers to how important a brand is to us, how intertwined it is in our lives. Brands need to matter to our personal lives. The more brands matter, the greater the neural activation they elicit, and vice versa. We cannot yet say which comes first, the neural activation or the brand association, but we can measure the amount of neural activation. This means that through neuroexperience, we now have a method to accurately measure "neuro brand share" – the magnitude of brain activation that is triggered when brands matter to us.

Remember that in Read Montague's unblinded taste test study (see page 153), where the subjects were told what they were about to taste, most chose Coke even if they might choose Pepsi on the basis of taste alone.[2] Montague explained that it was the Coke marketing might that had created stronger personal associations for the subjects. Thus Coke had more relevance than Pepsi, and this relevance was registered and observed in the subjects' brain scans. Montague states that brands are relevant to the degree to which they activate the dopaminergic[3] reward systems of the brain which are involved in creating feelings of pleasure or motivation.

Brand coherence refers to the likelihood that a brain region is activated in a way proportional to the degree to which that region has been specifically activated by the brand's cues in the past. Cues then are of central importance to brands. These cues should be repeated, and they must be specific. Repetition builds memories. Specificity means that the cues have defined associations. In neuroexperience terms, coherence means that cues repeatedly activate the same brain real estate. Coherence, then, is repeated specificity.

Martin Lindstrom in his best-selling book *Buyology* (2009) writes about the marketing programs of many tobacco companies that must now rely almost entirely on subtle cues for their branding. These companies have been forced to rely on the power of subtle cues that affect the subconscious. These cues are specific in their association to a brand such as Marlboro, and the company has used repetition of these cues in controlled settings like hotels. He writes:

> Thanks to worldwide bans on tobacco advertising on television, in magazines, and just about everywhere else, cigarette companies including Philip Morris, which manufactures Marlboro, and the R.J. Reynolds Tobacco Company,

---

2 As reported in Clive Thompson, "There's a sucker born in every medial prefrontal cortex," *New York Times*, October 2003: http://www.nytimes.com/2003/10/26/magazine/26BRAINS.html?ex=1068147831&ei=1&en (accessed May 18, 2010).

3 Dopamine is a neurotransmitter – one of the chemicals neurons use to speak to each other. It has been hypothesized that dopamine plays a major role in transmitting reward predictions.

which owns Camel, funnel a huge percentage of their marketing budget into this kind of subliminal brand exposure. Philip Morris, for example, offers bar owners financial incentives to fill their venues with color schemes, specifically designed furniture, ashtrays, suggestive tiles designed in captivating shapes similar to parts of the Marlboro logo, and other subtle symbols that, when combined, convey the very essence of Marlboro – without even the mention of the brand name or sight of the an actual logo. These "installations", or "Marlboro Motels" as they're known in the business, usually consist of lounge areas filled with comfy Marlboro red sofas positioned in front of TV screens spooling scenes of the Wild West – with its rugged cowboys, galloping horses, wide open spaces, and red sunsets all designed to evoke the essence of the iconic "Marlboro Man.

Brand richness refers to the likelihood that a particular piece of brain real estate will engage in a way directly related to the number of links it has with other regions that are also activated by the brand. Richness is akin to amplification. The more neurons are activated and interacting with each other, the richer the brand – the more it is amplified at the relevant brain address. Generally, the richness effect is at work when brands build an engaging experience around the brand that invokes all of the senses.

Apple creates such an experience in its Apple shops. Customers are not just presented with Apple products as they would be in more traditional shops. Instead, customers get to interact with the products, attend usability lectures, and so on. All of this helps deepen the richness of the Apple brand. National Geographic has applied the same richness principle in the design of its flagship stores. These are not just places to buy products, they evoke a certain lifestyle and attitude. The National Geographic store in London is part art gallery, part retail shop, part café, and part history lesson. There the clothes are displayed on bureaux from China or hospital stretchers that were actually used in the Vietnam war. All this adds to the richness of the experience. The end result is a cacophony of brain activity at the relevant brain address, which leads to brand building.

Walcot's three laws may already be known to marketers out there. However, neuroexperience provides a way for business managers to quantify and even predict the probability of success of an organization's Customer Experience and branding efforts.

Organizations can use these findings to great effect. It is often expensive to test real-world pilots of new products and services. One way to overcome this is to create the prototypes virtually, then have customers interact with them while being brain scanned. Think of it as having a replica virtual safari while lying prone in an fMRI scanner. The scans will reveal whether the appropriate brain real estate is being activated. What neuroexperience pioneers are establishing is a neuromap for brand success. They are plotting the Neuropoly game board in a step-by-step fashion. Perhaps as we perfect this methodology, the likes of Frito-Lay (see page 154) will not have to rely on biometrics, neuro-experience's first cousin, as a proxy.

The story of course does not end with the neural mechanics of how customers respond to marketing. There has been a tremendous amount of interest in how we make tough decisions. A tough decision is any one where there is a tradeoff to be had. We described this as dissonance earlier. Examples of tradeoffs include:

- going to the gym or not
- investing in that "get rich quick" scheme or not
- clicking on that Facebook application that asks you to sign up or not
- agreeing to participate in a marketing survey for a coupon or not
- paying down a loan a year early or not.

Neuroeconomics is the field that has taken on these challenges. Neuro-economics combines psychology, economics, and neuroscience, to study how people make decisions. It looks at the role of the brain when we evaluate decisions, categorize risks and rewards, and interact with each other. Neuroeconomics has proven to be a sharp turn in economics thinking.

The traditional approach in economics is based on the assumption of the rational being, a fundamental mistake. That is, there is an assumption that we as individuals behave according to logical principles. It is assumed that we rationally weigh the available information and make appropriate decisions accordingly. In other words, the assumptions one makes in economics are crucial. Theories based on these assumptions are useful, but if we are to predict human decisions we need a way to understand how we really make decisions, not just how we theoretically make those decisions.

The traditional field of economics has the same basic flaw as the traditional view of customer experience. Traditional economics formally declares that only the conscious rational world matters. Neuro-economics throws that notion on its head, and demonstrates the existence and power of the subconscious and emotional world in our decision making.

Neuroeconomics has two major foundations: first, prospect theory via behavioral economics, and second, neuroscience. Behavioral economics is a descriptive approach to economics that is concerned with how decisions are actually made, while traditional economics is a prescriptive approach concerned with how decisions *should be* made.

Behavioral economics has come to the fore in the last few years. In fact, the 2002 Nobel Prize in economics was awarded to Daniel Kahneman for his pioneering work in this area. The theory he developed along with Amos Tversky is called prospect theory.

Prospect theory and all of economics are shorthand for understanding what we value. To put it simply, economics is the science of understanding what we do to gain value or to avoid losing value. Prospect theory is the major theory of behavioral economics that has at its core the notion that our value calculations are not wholly rational in reality! The beauty of prospect theory for economists is that it can be explained mathematically. This means its principles can be documented, debated, and tested. Our purpose here is not to explain prospect theory, but rather to briefly highlight the fact that it is one of the two foundations of neuroeconomics. Behavioral economics and prospect theory demonstrate that business people are required to go beyond the rational to explain how customers actually make decisions.

Emotional decisions

The other foundation, of course, is neuroscience. What then is the neuroexperience of decision making as we do it in reality? Thomas Damasio developed a view based on neuroscientific evidence that explains "emotional decision making." Damasio's theory is called the somatic marker hypothesis, and is summarized in his book *Descartes' Error* (1994). You may recall Descartes' famous statement:

I think, therefore I am.

Well, Damasio would likely say:

I feel, therefore I exist.

Damasio and others had observed the following:

■ People who had damage to a particular area of the brain exhibited severely impaired decision making, especially for social behaviors.
■ The social decision making was most defective in interpersonal relationships and things requiring financial judgments.
■ These same people had normal intellectual abilities but impaired emotional behavior.

These findings led Damasio to the conclusion that emotion plays a

168

central role in decision making via the brain. Emotions can play a role consciously (in our gut feeling), or subconsciously (for instance, through biases). Different brain real estate is involved in gut feeling effects versus bias effects. Neuroeconomics explores the neural root cause of these non-rational (gut feeling or bias) aspects of decision making.

Patrick Renvoise and Christophe Morin have given perhaps the simplest description:

> Researchers have demonstrated that human beings make decisions in an emotional manner and then justify them rationally. Furthermore, we know that the final decision is actually triggered by the old brain, a brain that doesn't even understand words.
>
> P. Renvoise and C. Morin, *Neuromarketing* (2007)

Let's look at one study to get a glimpse of the power of neuro-economics. Many scenarios exist that cannot be accounted for by rational economic theory. Two examples are:

■ Employees are willing to forgo part of their salary if they believe that their employer's mission is valuable (that is, praiseworthy rather than profitable). These employees are willing to make a sacrifice (pay a premium) in order to work for the organization.
■ Customers choose a less convenient store simply because they do not like the policies of the nearest store. These customers are making a sacrifice in time and convenience to do business with the less convenient store.

Delgado and Dilmore conducted a neuroeconomics study to explore this type of situation with a trust game.[4] Subjects were given a dollar and told that they had a choice:

■ Keep the dollar outright (that is, gain a financial value of $1).
■ Share the money with a fictional partner. If shared, the money would be tripled and the partner could then share the $3 with the subject. However, the partner could also decide to keep the $3 at that point, leaving the subject with nothing.

The subject did not see the partner but was given a briefing about

---

4 M. R. Delgado and J. G. Dilmore, Social and emotional influences on decision making and the brain, *Minnesota Journal of Law, Science and Technology*, 9(2), 2008.

them. Three different partners profiles were created by Delgao and Dilmore:

- The *moral partner* was described as having saved a woman from a fire at a club.
- The *neutral partner* was described as having missed taking a flight that crashed.
- The *immoral partner* was described as a business school graduate who tried to sell heating panels from the space shuttle *Columbia* on the internet.

The experiment was set up such that each fictional partner rewarded the subject 50 percent of the time regardless of the partner's description. Each subject played 24 rounds of the game with each of the fictional partners. The behavioral findings are fascinating:

- Pre-experiment the subjects rated the fictional partners in line with their descriptions. That is, the ratings of each partner were hierarchical and in line with the "moral"-sounding fortitude of the partners. The moral partner was rated highest at the start, and the immoral partner was rated the lowest (not surprising).
- Post-experiment the subjects rated the fictional partners as about the same as each other. After all, the partners all rewarded the subjects at the same 50 percent rate (so perhaps this too was not surprising).
- Nevertheless, during game play, the subjects trusted the moral partner more than the immoral partner. This behavior was consistent throughout the game (SURPRISING).

So even though the subjects, first, consciously rated the partners differentially at the beginning before they could experience the partner's behavior, and second, consciously rated the partners the same at the conclusion of the 24 trials, the subjects' behavior did not match their conscious assessment. Something else was obviously at play. The emotive connection of the partner description overrode the subject's conscious judgment!

The fMRI scans of the subjects showed equally fascinating results.

- A brain area that is involved in rewards behavior (the striatum) was activated when learning whether the neutral partner was going to share, as this information was being used by the subject for future game decisions (not surprising).
- In fact, activity in this brain structure was increased when the

neutral partner shared and decreased when the neutral partner kept the whole $3 (not surprising).

■ However, the fMRI showed vastly different neuroexperience when the subjects played the game with the moral and immoral partners. In these cases the brain's reward center showed no differential activation.

Delgado and Dilmore explain that:

> This suggests that the brain's trial and error learning system may have been inhibited during the game by the availability of prior information. Participants may have bypassed the current feedback (eg, [moral] partner did not share with me on this trial) due to the overwhelming prior social information. Consequently, subjects did not update their decision-making, preferring instead to conform to their original biases created by irrational social expectations.

The potential implications for organizations become immediately clear. Qaalfa often states that "One of the key outcomes of providing a great Customer Experience is that customers become willing to pay a premium (for instance in time, money, or reduction in quality) to do business with you." If the organization delivers a relevant, coherent, and rich neuroexperience, the business may be awarded an override in the customer's brain! The override says, "Forget that at this particular time you are not getting the best deal in rational terms. You have previous Customer Experience information to best guide your decision making."

Predicting decisions

Several times we have mentioned that part of the power of neuro-experience will be in its ability to more accurately predict behavior and attitudes. Prediction of behavior is already being studied. Knutson and colleagues published a classic fMRI paper describing how neural activity could predict purchases.[5] Figure 10.1 highlights their study design and findings.

Subjects were scanned while they were being presented with a series of purchase decisions. Prior to the purchase choice, subjects were first presented with an image of the product, immediately followed by another image of the product with its associated price. After the completion of one purchase decision, the subject was asked to fixate on

---

5 B. Knutson, S. Rick, E. Wimmer, D. Prelec, and G. Loewenstein, Neural predictors of purchases, *Neuron* 53, January 2007.

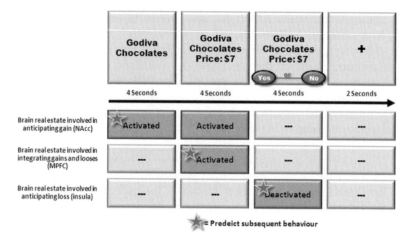

Figure 10.1 Research on how neural activity could predict purchases

cross-hairs prior to the start of the next trial. This last step is like eating a cracker in-between wine tastings.

The researchers found that it is possible to predict behavior based on the neuroexperience. More specifically they found that the following brain activations each predicted purchase behavior:

- Activation of brain real estate (nucleus accumbens) involved in anticipating gain during the product phase significantly predicts purchase behavior.
- Activation of brain real estate (mesial pre-frontal cortex) involved in integrating loss and gain information during the choice phase significantly predicts purchase behavior.
- Deactivation of brain real estate that is involved in assessing losses (insula) during the purchase phase significantly predicts subsequent purchase decisions.

These findings show that prediction of behavior is a realistic use of neuroexperience, although it's still early days for this as a practical tool for businesses. It is exciting to think of the experiments that will be coming that seek to expand our prediction ability. In time, researchers will begin to look at the temporal relationship between neural precursors and purchase decisions. That is to say, researchers will in time begin to unravel which brain structure's neural activity is a precursor of purchase decisions one minute, one hour, one day, or one week before a purchase decision is made. The power of neuroeconomics is that we are getting to a point where we will be able to predict trade-off decision behavior based on brain activity.

As our neuroexperience knowledge expands, the questions we have and the studies researchers would like to run get more sophisticated and naturalistic. One advancement in fMRI helps us use the technique under more social conditions. The technique was developed by Read Montague, who heads up the Brown Human Neuroimaging Laboratory at Baylor College of Medicine in Houston, Texas. As part of our continuous efforts to stay at the cutting edge of thought leadership in Customer Experience, Qaalfa visited Read in the impressive lab he's put together in Houston. Qaalfa lays the groundwork:

> It's been a while since I studied neuropsychology. Back then, PET scans had only been used for diagnostic purposes in humans for about 10 years. At the time I was interested in the differential diagnosis of Alzheimers based on the mathematical analysis of CT and PET scans. fMRI did not even exist yet. I then moved into management and left the clinical research behind.
>
> As neuroscience began to make it headway into Customer Experience, I began to refresh myself with the developments in the area. I knew there were two people I really wanted to speak with: Gemma Calvert and Read Montague, two heavyweights in the fMRI world. Gemma is based just down the road from our UK offices, and Read is based in my home town, Houston, Texas.
>
> They do everything large in Texas, and I knew Read's operation was going to be impressive. Read's lab did not disappoint on that front. He has several fMRI scanners dedicated to non-clinical research. This is amazing especially given that his lab is based in a medical school.
>
> I met a couple of his students, and one in particular, Ann Harvey (who received her Ph.D. the very next week), was particularly impressive. I am sure she will be a name to be reckoned with in the world of neuroexperience.
>
> I basically wanted to know how they saw applied fMRI from their vantage point. what they thought is the future of computational neuroscience. Suffice it to say that Read's vision of the future is not limited to customer neuroexperience. He makes the case in his book, *Why Buy This Book? How we make decisions* (2006), that all that we do is ultimately dependent on the binary-like computations that occur in the brain. I suggest you give Read's book a try (especially if you have previous exposure to neuroscience). Read's thoughts are fascinating.
>
> As for everyone else in neuroexperience, the key tool available to Read is the fMRI. His lab is full of them. Traditional fMRI is limited to scanning a single individual in isolation. As a result, fMRI studies must be designed with this limitation in mind. Read developed hyperscanning as a workaround for this problem. It is the simultaneous joining of two or more fMRI scanners so that the subjects can interact with one another in real time while they are being scanned. This means that more naturalistic experiments can be carried out.

This is a brilliant development for neuroexperience. As Montague and his colleagues point out:

> Two subjects could compete against each other in a digital video game, controlled remotely by an experimenter. Each time a move is made, the brain of the subject making the move is scanned, while the brain of the subject watching the move is simultaneously scanned.[6]

Hyperscanning makes it possible to studying scenarios in order to understand the neuroexperience of both parties during, for example:

■ a call center interaction
■ an internet chat
■ a performance feedback session between manager and employee.

In hyperscanning, the actual fMRI scanners are the same as in single-person fMRI. The advancement comes in the software that controls the machine. Hyperscanning allows one researcher to control multiple fMRI scanners no matter where they are located. For example, a researcher in Houston could control scanners in London, New York City, Tokyo, and Sydney simultaneously. The software allows the subjects to react to the stimuli and to each other.

Kings-Casa and colleagues used hyperscanning to further investigate the neuroexperience of trust in a more naturalistic social scenario.[7] The concept of trust between people requires the ability to investigate a complex human relationship.

For example, in a game in which two players send money back and forth with risk, trust is operationalized as the amount of money a sender gives to a receiver without external enforcement. Such trust games now enjoy widespread use in both experimental economics and neuroscience experiments.

The set-up of the Kings-Casa study is similar to that in the single-person trust game described previously, in which the investor's brain was scanned while a fictional partner shared money 50 percent of the time. However, in this study:

■ the investor could invest any portion of $20 with the partner
■ the money was then increased threefold by the experimenter

---

6 P. R. Montague, G. S. Berns, J. D. Cohen, et al., Hyperscanning: Simultaneous fMRI during linked social interactions. *NeuroImage* 16(4), 2002.

7 B. Kings-Casa, D. Tomlin D, A. Anen C. Camerer, S. Quartz, and R. Montague, Getting to know you: Reputation and trust in a two-person economic exchange, *Science*, 308, April 2005.

- then the partner then decided how much of the tripled amount to repay to the investor
- a game included series of these trials in succession
- the hyperscans of investor and partner were studied to determine whether the partner's decision could be predicted over the series of trials.

In the end, based only on the neuroexperience evidence, the partner's decision could accurately be predicted 14 seconds ahead of time. In other words there was a 14-second neuroexperience lead time. Fourteen seconds may seem meager to you, but this lead time shows that neuro-experience prediction is possible. Future neuroexperience studies will allow us to predict behavior with even greater lead times.

The greater the trust lead time, the stronger the trust relationship. This is a useful measure, and relevant to business today. Trust is a type of premium. It is a risk taken on the part of customers. It would be very useful if a business could extend trust lead time. It represents a reduction in cost to sale in subsequent customer interactions.

So where does this leave us? Joseph LeDoux in his book *The Emotional Brain* (1996) states that "A major goal of modern brain science is to figure out in as much detail as possible where different functions live in the brain, Knowing where a function is located is the first step toward understanding how it works." We are on our way, as the studies highlighted above demonstrate. However, as with any new science and paradigm shift, there are waving warning flags. There are always misrepresentations and outright charlatans ready to take advantage of the unsuspecting. There are also the fearmongers and naysayers to contend with.

It is worth mentioning a couple of cautions. There is a reason we have used terms like "oversimplify" to describe much of the popular writing on neuroexperience for a novice audience. It is important to keep in mind that much of the richness of what is known today is lost when one purposefully strips out all accurate technical reference to neuroanatomy, neurochemistry, and neurophysiology. This desalination of the neuroscience behind the concepts presented here makes the overall neuroexperience message palatable, but it also neuters much of the practicality of the underlying mechanisms. There is absolutely nothing wrong with keeping it simple, as long as you keep in mind that we are doing just that.

There is also the other side of this coin, where neuroscience terms are strewn about for their effect when in reality the emperor wears no clothes. A March 2008 Neurosciencemarketing.com/blog[8] states

---

8 http://www.neurosciencemarketing.com/blog/articles/neuromarketing-blog-my-secret-revealed.htm (accessed May 18, 2010).

that "We've all seen research that arrives at bland, inconsequential, or inconclusive findings but seems credible and useful because these findings were produced using advanced neuroscience technology – we all need to make the effort to set aside the neuroscientific trappings of research and focus on provable results."

Keeping these cautions in mind, let's summarize the key points we have outlined:

■ Neuroexperience is a burgeoning field focused on the experience the customer has at the neuro-anatomical, neurophysical, neuro-chemical, and neurophysiological levels. This experience often occurs subconsciously, and is the result of interaction/(s) between an organization and a customer.

■ The ultimate aim in understanding the customer neuroexperience is to approach neuropoly, the Holy Grail of neuroexperience. Neuropoly is the neuroexperience state where the organization is, first, optimally activating areas of the brain modulating the positive emotions known to drive business value, while at the same, second, minimizing or inhibiting the activation of brain systems that are responsible for the emotions that destroy business value.

■ The key neuroexperience metric will be "share of brain."

■ The "neuro-" prefix is becoming pervasive, indicating that society is becoming more accustomed to neurological concepts and modes of explanation.

■ The main tool employed in current neuroexperience studies is fMRI.

■ Brand powerhouses and visionary companies have already started to apply neuromarketing as a source of competitive advantage.

■ Neuroexperience findings have identified three branding laws that help companies achieve neuropoly. Brands need to relevant, coherent, and rich.

■ It is possible to predict behavior accurately based on neuroexperience findings, although at this point the prediction lead times are short.

■ There are a couple of neuroexperience fMRI studies that you might find it worth considering having carried out for your organization today:

● Competitive neurobranding – presenting your and competitive brands to customers to see how different the fMRI activation is. The results of this study can tell you how different your brand is perceived to be from competitive ones. You will also get information on which broad emotions are involved. Ultimately this will tell you how close your business is to achieving neuropoly versus the competition. The finding of interest is the differential magnitude effect of neural activation between the brands.

- Brand trust – using a standard fMRI, you can play a trust game with your customer. You explain to the customer that they have some cash to share with one of two fictional partners, including a branded partner, described in a way that ensures brand associations are prominent in their profile. The neutral partner has no such brand mentions in their profile. Each of the partners will share with the customer at the same 50 percent rate. You are looking for differences in the sharing behavior of the customer throughout the game. If your brand has positive associations, you will find that the customer shares with the branded partner more than with the neutral partner.

■ Two leading fMRI practitioners, trusted names to consult, are Gemma Calvert, based in the United Kingdom, and Read Montague, based in the United States.

- The Human Neuroimaging Laboratory is part of the Department of Neuroscience at Baylor College of Medicine, and is headed by Read Montague. It has particular interest in "hyperscanning (a means of exploring the brain activity that underlies human social interactions), social neuroscience, neural circuitry of valuation and decision-making, and disruptions of such processes associated with developmental and psychiatric illness."

- The Applied Neuroimaging Group at Warwick University's Digital Lab is led by Professor Gemma Calvert, and seeks "to apply techniques developed from the field of cognitive neuroscience to help industry better understand the consumer's brain. With over 10 years experience in neuromarketing, the group combines expertise in the techniques of functional magnetic resonance imaging (fMRI), psychophysics and electroencephalography (EEG) to help marketers, advertisers and manufacturers with new product development, effective communication and prediction of consumer behaviour."

■ Of course there are other sources of information. Here are a few academic-based research centers, with brief descriptions based on information provided on their websites:

- Rangel Neuroeconomics lab at Stanford University, headed by Antonio Rangel. Its mission is "to study the computational and neurobiological basis of value-based decision-making using tools from cognitive neuroscience (fMRI, transcranial magnetic stimulation, and eye tracking) and experimental economics."

- The Center for the Study of Neuroeconomics at George Mason University, headed by Kevin McCabe. "The center is dedicated to the experimental study of how emergent mental computations in the brain interact with the emergent computations of institutions to produce legal, political, and economic order."

- The Center for Neuroeconomics at New York University, headed by Paul Glimcher, "is one of the preeminent institutions for the study of decision making and the brain. The Center brings together faculty and students from NYU's world-class departments of Neural Science, Economics, and Psychology in classes, seminars and research groups. Working with techniques ranging from single neuron electrophysiology to traditional experimental economics to functional brain imaging, more than a dozen research groups at NYU seek to understand the neurobiological basis of choice. New York University: The Center for Neuroeconomics has formed there."

- The Neuroeconomics Lab at the University of Bonn, located at the Life and Brain Research Center headed by Bernd Weber. "The interdisciplinary research team of neuroscientists, psychologists and economists will study the neurophysiological basis of economic decision making by applying neuroimaging techniques as well as classical experimental economics."

- The Center for Neuropolicy at Emory University, headed by Gregory S. Berns, "will focus on how the biology of the brain influences decision-making in politics, policy and business. As a partnership among researchers in the Emory School of Medicine, Emory College and the Goizueta Business School, the center will create an ideal environment to accelerate discovery in this emerging field."

- The Erasmus Centre for Neuroeconomics, headed by Ale Smidts, "brings together expertise in economics, psychology, and neuroscience with the aim of contributing to a neuroeconomics theory of human behaviour. The ECN enjoys excellent collaboration with the Donders Institute for Brain, Cognition and Behaviour at the Radboud University in the Netherlands, with access to their world-class neuroimaging facilities."

We have covered quite some territory. We started with a brief trip around the brain, went onto the streets for a virtual neuroexperience safari, and finished with look into the future of neuroexperience.

Now let's ground ourselves in the state of today's Customer Experience. If you are thinking of dipping your organization's proverbial toe in any of the "emerging trends" waters, you will find it useful to arm yourself with a few experience gap statistics. Even if you are still firmly on the sidelines, the experience gaps outlined in our final chapter will prove interesting.

11 And so in summary ...

I cannot change yesterday. I can make the most of today and look with hope towards tomorrow.

Anon

From the heady heights of neuroexperience and our revealing what a potential future could look like, we come down with a bit of a bump to this summary. Our intention is to familiarize you in the reality of today, and give you an assessment of where the Customer Experience is today and what you need to do. As we mentioned in Chapter 1, every six months we conduct a survey and then webinar on what we call the Customer Experience Tracker. The survey looks at the state of the Customer Experience as measured by businesses and customers. There are a few interesting results that we think are relevant as we close this book.

In Figure 11.1 you can see 14 of the 20 emotions that drive or

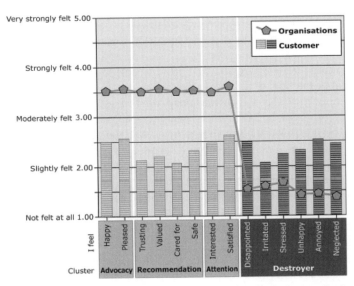

Figure 11.1 How customers feel towards organizations, and what organizations think their customers feel towards them

179

destroy value we have discussed before. We can see how organizations think they are performing on a scale of 0 to 10, and how customers think they are performing. There appears to be a significant gap! Clearly organizations are fooling themselves and believe they are a lot better than they actually are. This gap shows us there is a lack of understanding of how to build an emotionally engaging experience.

Qaalfa explains how the impact of this gap played out at board level with one of our clients:

> It was a fairly healthy looking business on paper. The board was in the enviable position of being able to make moves pretty much unencumbered by other voices. Even more spectacular was that the Chief Commercial Officer called me and said he was worried about the way things were going. While his short-term figures were more or less positive, he saw that customer satisfaction was never impacted by anything they did. They increased the number of customer-facing people by 10 percent – no change. They discounted prices on some key products – no change. They invested heavily in service development – no change. Basically, no matter what they did, customer satisfaction seemed to be unchanged. This worried the CMO because he thought it might mean:
> - customers are truly satisfied and we have true loyalty
> - our satisfaction scores are erroneous
> - our satisfaction scores are not the right measure to tell us how customers think of us.
>
> The problem was that he was not confident which of these it was. He was worried that the company was effectively blinding itself with its own customer research. To be sure his Director of Customer Research assured him that all was well.
>
> He called me and asked how he might be able to look into the situation to get at the true, or at least an alternative, picture of customer thinking. You now know that the answer today could be investigated using experience psychology, social media, or neuroexperience. We used some simply employed experience psychology techniques. The bottom line was that we found customers were developing a deep-seated hatred (and yes, I mean hatred) of the experience the company was delivering. They felt the company had the best products and decent prices. They simply were waiting for the time when a competitor developed the ability offer something similar. The CCO's read of the situation was apt. Had he waited, a tipping point would have been reached whereby a critical mass of customers could have bolted for the first competitor within shouting distance. The point is that it is sometimes necessary to check yourself, even when all the customary evidence and experts suggest that things are all right. In order to see the customer – to truly "see" the customer – you need to use different lenses to make sure you do not come to believe in illusions.

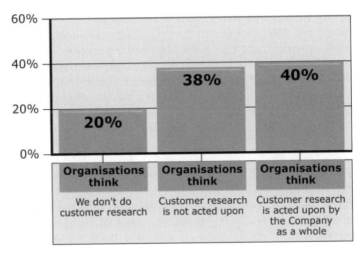

Figure 11.2 The extent to which customer research findings are acted on

However, conducting research is only part of the jigsaw. Once conducted it needs to be acted upon. Again from the Customer Experience Tracker, you can see in Figure 11.2 that some 20 percent of organizations do not undertake any form of customer research! What do they do – guess what customers want? This is one of the indicators we use to see how customer-centric an organization is. Also 38 percent of organizations do not act upon the research that is undertaken. They commit the time, energy, and resource to undertake the work, and then do nothing.

Colin reflects on the first few days he had as VP of Customer Experience at BT, and provides an example of this:

I remember in the first few days of being promoted to VP, Customer Experience, I attended a feedback session on annual customer research someone had commissioned on the services that we provided. This was the third or fourth time this research had been undertaken over as many years.

As I listened to the agency presenter, I was surprised by her attitude. It was very matter of fact. She clearly did not want to be there. She came across as if this was a waste of her time. Halfway through I stopped the presentation and challenged her on her attitude. I said, "Why are you delivering this presentation like you don't care?"

"Don't care?" she said. "I don't care!" She smiled as if to say that was ironic. Clearly, I had hit on a raw nerve! She continued, "We have been undertaking this research for you for the last three or four years. Each year we tell you that your customers are unhappy with the service you provide, and they want you to change it. Each year people sit here and nod in agreement, and then guess what: nothing happens. Therefore, the following year we do the same research, which tells you the same thing. The only change is it's just got worse. Again people nod and nothing happens! So with respect, it is not that I don't care, it is that you don't care. You don't care that customer service is getting worse. What I really don't understand is why you waste your money in doing this research if you are only going to ignore it!"

I was taken aback by her outburst, but could understand her frustration. To be honest, she was right. We didn't care. We just did research, as that is often what big companies do.

In my new role I went about changing this, and I am proud to say we had some great results, as the market was crying out for these changes. It was, however, a major internal challenge to do this. The reality was that senior execs were more worried about cutting costs than improving the Customer Experience. Yes, they said the words, but when it came down to it, cost savings always won the day. They might have not admitted that, but their actions spoke volumes. After a number of failed attempts to get funding to change things, based on this research, I realized that I was going about it in the wrong way. I was going to the senior execs with a case to improve the Customer Experience. I realized that if they were only interested in cost savings, I needed to present the case based on how many cost savings we could make. As we investigated the situation, we uncovered huge costs that were being driven into the business from the poor service. We then presented a case based on how much money we could save. Eureka – it was passed! Sometimes you need to speak the language that is most acceptable.

What is the issue here? We assume the reason you have read this book is that you are interested in the topic. We hope we have enlightened you along the way. However, what we do know is that to understand customer requirements is only half the battle. The other half of the battle, and the more important one, is to get people to stand up, take notice, and actually DO something.

Since 2002, we have had the pleasure of working with a number of CEOs and their teams across many different industry sectors around the globe from our offices in London and Atlanta, USA. Over the years, sadly, we have found that only 20 percent of CEOs and their teams are really committed to improving their Customer Experience and making their organizations customer-centric. The other 80 percent fall into two groups.

Forty percent say they support a new customer initiative, but they are not committed. You can see it in their actions. Typically the signs are:

ot being available to discuss implicationsanting to spend limited time on strategyot being actively involvedack of understanding of the implicationsnly speaking "inside out" language, which focuses on what isood for the companyll examples are "inside out," with no customer storiesimited time spent with customers.hese are just a few of the signs. I know that CEOs and their teamsre busy people, but if this is a key initiative, it deserves their time, ase are normally talking about changing the culture of a company, andulture change starts at the top.

Sadly, the final 40 percent could not care less, and any initiative isoomed to failure from the start.

We have a policy of challenging all of our clients at the beginning ofny engagement by asking, "Are you serious?" Our advice is very direct.f they are not, then we do not waste their time or effort. Surprise,urprise: the engagements that work are the ones where people areerious.

It is not a matter, though, of simply asking people whether they areerious. As one client put it, "What senior executive in their right mindould say the customers are not important?" You need to hear themnd see their actions, or lack of actions.

Bruce Temkin, a leading industry thought leader, wrote an excellentlog.[1] Bruce's insights on the key role of CEOs in Customer Experi-nce are spot on. It went a long way in articulating our thoughts onhe subject of getting CEOs and their teams involved.he focus on customer experience must come from the CEO'slear belief that it impacts business results. It is a core businessmperative, not a "nice to have" initiative.ince customer experience provides real financial benefits, it'sorthy of investment. The CEO's willingness to invest in thesereas is a clear signal to the organization that customer experiencexcellence is critical; not just an empty slogan.eople focus on what's measured, incentivized, and celebrated.o embed customer experience within the core operating fabricf a company, therefore, firms need to refine what it measures,ncentivizes, and celebrates. So make sure that your HR exec isnvolved in the customer experience effort.ny customer experience transformation needs to be driven by

---

1 Bruce Temkin, <http://experiencematters.wordpress.com/>.

the voice of the customer; so CEOs should look for a customer experience dashboard with a handful of customer metrics (like satisfaction or Net Promoter). And hold your entire executive team accountable for improving those metrics; don't offload the responsibility to a chief customer officer.

■ This effort requires active involvement and commitment by the CEO. Why? Because transformation efforts can easily get bogged down in politics and silos. So reviewing progress of the firm's customer experience efforts needs to become a regular part of the executive agenda.

To Bruce's points we would add a few more:

■ People need to "get it." The concepts behind the Customer Experience, particularly that over 50 percent of an experience is about emotions, are not accepted instantly by people in organizations. The CEO needs to realize that time and patience are the order of the day.

■ After time has been spent coaching and showing people how to become more customer-focused, if someone still refuses to buy in to this new thinking, the CEO needs to remove that person. This will also send a strong message to everyone else in the organization.

■ The CEO must talk about customers constantly, visit customers frequently, and listen to customers, making changes as a result of the feedback.

■ Most importantly, the CEO must tell customer stories. These bring to life the effect the organization is having on customers.

■ Be bold! Barry Judge and Best Buy have been bold with the introduction of Twelpforce. They admitted it is a very "public experiment." Don't be scared to try something new.

■ Finally and most importantly, if the CEO and their team are not serious, don't bother. It will do more harm than good if they start down this path in a half-hearted manner.

We hope this helps. We would suggest that if your CEO and their team are not operating in this manner, you should somehow make sure they see this book. Maybe, just maybe, it will help them realize what they need to change. However, be aware that improving the Customer Experience is not easy. If it was, everyone would be doing it, and we would have great experiences all the time. But also be clear: the prize is well worth the effort. Thomas Edison's famous quote comes to mind:

Opportunity is missed by most people because it is dressed in overalls and looks like work.

Are you going to miss this opportunity to move your organization's Customer Experience further? Are you going to miss the opportunity to improve your Customer Experience? Surely the answer must be no. We know this work is very gratifying. To actually change an organization, to change the Customer Experience, to make your customers happy, is surely a battle worth fighting.

We wish you well in your quest. Please don't be a stranger: the three of us are on Twitter, LinkedIn, and blog regularly – we would welcome a chat with you at any time. Good luck!

	Twitter	**Linked in**
Colin Shaw	@ColinShaw_CX	http://uk.linkedin.com/pub/colin-shaw/0/118/85b
Qaalfa Dibeehi	@QaalfaDibeehi	http://uk.linkedin.com/pub/qaalfa-dibeehi/0/81/371
Steven Walden	@Steven_Walden	http://uk.linkedin.com/pub/steven-walden/0/999/18a

Web & Blog: www.beyondphilosophy.com

References

Note: details are given here of books mentioned in the text. See the footnotes for details of articles and other sources.

Damasio, T. (1994) *Descartes' Error: Emotion, reason and the human brain*, London: Penguin Books.

Gladwell, M. (2006) *Blink: The power of thinking without thinking*, London: Penguin Books.

Hamel, G. and Prahalad, C. K. (1994) *Competing for the Future*, Boston, Mass.: Harvard Business School Press.

Kluger, J. (2009) *Your Brain: A user's guide*, New York: Time Books.

LeDoux, J. (1996) *The Emotional Brain*, New York: Simon & Schuster.

Lindstrom, M (2010) *Buyology: Truth and lies about why we buy*, paperback edn, New York: Broadway.

Montague, R. (2006) *Why Choose this Book? How we make decisions*, New York: Dutton.

Pine, J. and Gilmore, J. (1999) *The Experience Economy*, Boston, Mass.: Harvard Business School Press.

Plous, S. (1993) *The Psychology of Judgement and Decision-Making*, New York: McGraw-Hill.

Renvoise, P. and Morin, C. (2007) *Neuromarketing: Understand the buy buttons in your customer's brain*, London: Nelson.

Shaw, C. (2004) *Revolutionize Your Customer Experience*, Basingstoke: Palgrave Macmillan.

Shaw, C. (2007) *The DNA of Customer Experience: How emotions drive and destroy value*, Basingstoke: Palgrave Macmillan.

Underhill, P. (2008) *Why We Buy: The science of shopping*, rev. edn, New York: Simon & Schuster.

Index